The OPEN ROAD'S BEST OF

by Paris Permenter & John Bigley

Open Road Travel Guides
For the amount of time you really have for your trip!

Open Road Publishing

Open Road's new travel guides cut to the chase.
You don't need a huge travel encyclopedia – you need a *selective guide* to steer you right. If you're going on vacation for a few weeks or less, get a guide that brings you the *best* of any destination for the amount of time you *really* have for your trip.
And get a guide that gives you all this for the *best price* around!

Open Road – the *affordable* guide you need for the trip you want.

The New Open Road *Best Of* Travel Guides.
To the point.
Uncluttered.
Easy.
Priced Right.

Open Road Publishing
P.O. Box 284, Cold Spring Harbor, NY 11724
www.openroadguides.com

Text Copyright © 2010 by Paris Permenter & John Bigley
- All Rights Reserved -
ISBN 13: 978-1-59360-137-9
ISBN 10: 1-59360-137-9
Library of Congress Control No. 200932494

For photo credits turn to page 8.

CONTENTS

PHOTO CREDITS

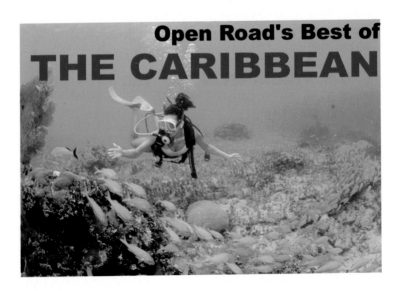

Open Road's Best of

THE CARIBBEAN

1. INTRODUCTION

Picture yourself on a tropical isle. Palm trees sway in the gentle breeze. Beyond a garden of blossoming bougainvillea and hibiscus, a fringe of powdery sand gives way to a sea as clear as white rum.

If this is your idea of paradise, as it is ours, then you're ready for the **Caribbean**. Whether you're headed to the tropics for a honeymoon, a long-deserved vacation, or a luxurious getaway, this guide is written for you. We'll take you to special places where vacationers feel not just welcomed but worshipped. Places where you can get away from the crowd on deserted beaches and in secluded inns or be part of the action in flashy casinos and red-hot nightspots. Destinations where you can spend your days scuba diving, exploring historic ruins, or shopping for duty-free goods from around the world or just hanging out in a hammock built for two.

Whether you are seeking a fiesta, siesta, or something in between, it's available in the Caribbean. You'll find that there's a wide array of vacation experiences awaiting you in the islands. Take your pick. Luxurious resorts where you can enjoy spa treatments during the day and casino gambling at night or small inns where you're part of a handful of guests. Fine gourmet meals enjoyed by candlelight or side-of-the-road discoveries that serve island specialties. Large islands that promise a peek at more history and culture around the next bend or small islands where you'll start seeing familiar faces within a few days. Add to this diversity a jigsaw of cultures, ranging from French to Dutch to

English, and you'll have a lifetime of vacation opportunities.

That smorgasbord of islands makes a guide like this one a necessity. Selecting an island, then narrowing down your choice of resorts and activities, is the first step in planning your romantic getaway. Once the choices are made, we'll help you decide how to get there, how to get around, and what to do. And we'll look at how to have fun, whether that means viewing marine life from 100 feet below the surface in a high-tech submarine or cruising down a Jamaican river on a bamboo raft. To help you bring back memories of your vacation, we'll shop for island specialties and duty-free treasures.

The islands and resorts covered here represent our personal picks. No doubt we have left out some hidden jewels. Unquestionably, there remain additional stretches of sand and hedonistic hideaways we've not discovered. But that's part of the fun for us as well. No Caribophile likes to think that he has seen the best of the best. It's better to dream that perhaps the pinnacle of palm tree-lined beaches and the ultimate in thatched roof beach bars lies beyond the next cove.

HOTEL & DINING COSTS IN THIS BOOK
Hotel (EP room-only) Resorts:
$ under $150 per room, per night, high season
$$ $151-$250 per room, per night, high season
$$$ $251-$350 per room, per night, high season
$$$$ over $350 per room, per night, high season

All-Inclusive Resorts
$ under $150 per person, per night, high season
$$ $151-$250 per person, per night, high season
$$$ $251-$350 per person, per night, high season
$$$$ over $350 per person, per night, high season

Restaurant Costs
$ under $15 per person
$$ $15-$30 per person
$$$ $31 and over per person

In the meantime, we've offered here our favorites, places where we know that you'll enjoy walking hand-in-hand and find yourself smiling for no reason at all. So grab your suitcase and a bottle of sunscreen, and let's go. It's a journey that will have us sampling different cultures, tasting new foods, enjoying beautiful resorts, and dancing under a starry sky. We'll travel to places where the nightlife is as hot as the daytime sun, to resorts where the boundaries between indoors and outdoors blur.

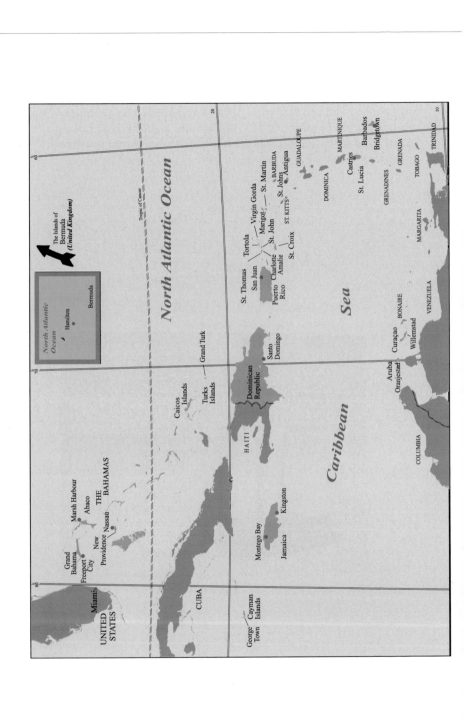

2. ANGUILLA

Travelers looking for the best the Caribbean has to offer—with the budget to back it up—often head to **Anguilla**. Home of exclusive resorts and world-class restaurants, this quiet island is a jetset favorite.

Anguilla is relatively small, so plan to have a look at most of the island during your stay. Getting around is easy—just stay on the main road to zip from end to end—and yet at the same time a little difficult because road signs are practically non-existent. Nonetheless, just about every road feeds off the main road so you can't go too far astray!

INTRO

The center of **Anguilla** is the location of the capital town (city would be an exaggeration) called **The Valley**. The community is home to government offices, the tourist board, the national museum, and several good restaurants. Unlike many Caribbean capitals, it is not located on the waterfront but near the island's highest point, **Crocus Hill**. Just south of The Valley sits **Wallblake Airport**, arrival point for many visitors.

South of The Valley runs **the main road** (yes, everyone just calls it "the main road"). It heads southwest of town through the village of George Hill and past the turnoff for **Sandy Ground Village**, the fishing and boating headquarters for the island. You'll find a good pullover on this stretch from which to look down on the town of Sandy Ground, a veritable strip of sand tucked between the bay and Road Salt Pond, from which islanders produced sea salt until a few years ago.

The main road continues southwest, traveling past a few houses sprinkled among the low growing vegetation. To the left at a traffic signal not far past the Sandy Ground turnoff lies the turn for **Blowing Point**, the ferry port that connect the island to nearby St. Martin.

Continuing west, the road reaches the island's top beaches and luxury resorts, the destination of many Anguilla vacationers. This area is also a stop for another kind of Anguilla vacationer—migrating birds. Salt ponds filled with brackish and salt water attract numerous birds to this region.

The **north end** of the island is also home to several good birding ponds. The north side is home to fewer guest accommodations (but a good destination for the traveler on a budget). Most travelers make the quick trip to this part of the island, however, for a look at its beaches.

Follow the main road through The Valley and past Stoney Ground then take a left at the fork to reach **Shoal Bay** (you'll see signs advertising beach bars and shops). This is one of the top beaches on the island and the most active beach for sunbathing and a little bar hopping. Other travelers take the right at the fork and continue on the main road to the next main fork, turning left to the community of **Island Harbour**, where many of the island's boats are built.

This is also the jump off point for nearby **Scilly Cay**, a popular afternoon excursion both for lunch and for snorkeling and sunbathing. From Island Harbour, follow the main road back around to The Valley. It's a quiet, winding drive that takes you past **The Copse**, the most tree-covered portion of the island.

The most economical transport around the island is a rental car. Taxi service, both in cars and 12-passenger vans, is available throughout the island. All taxis are on a call basis. You can ask for a taxi to be dispatched at the airport or the ferry port in Blowing Rock. Public transportation is not an option.

BEST SIGHTS IN ANGUILLA

SIGHTS

Anguilla is home to several small museums including the **National Trust** in The Valley, *Tel. 264/497-5297*, with local history exhibits plus several privately owned collections that welcome visitors.

The **Heritage Collection** (*Pond Ground, Tel. 264/497-4092*) is the work of Colville Petty, an authority on Anguilla's rich history. Housed in part of Petty's home, the museum spans the entire range of the island's history, from its Amerindian days to the 1967 Revolution. Check out the collection of **Arawak artifacts**, including an Arawak shell necklace, a hollowed conch shell that served as an early drinking vessel, and spindle whorls, used to spin cotton to make hammocks and religious symbols for the Arawaks are also on display. Talking to Colville Petty about the island's history is well worth the price of admission.

SPORTS & RECREATION

BEST SPORTS & RECREATION

Snorkeling and **diving** are also top pursuits. Anguilla is just making its move into the world of scuba diving and still offers pristine conditions around the island for those looking for adventure in the form of coral reef dives as well as wreck dives.

Some **popular dive sites** include:

• **Sandy Island**, 30-70 feet. A good site for sea fans and soft corals.

• **Sandy Deep**, 15-60 feet. A mini-wall offers divers the chance to spot hard corals, abundant fish life, and occasionally stingrays.

• **Aughor's Deep**, 110 feet. This deep dive includes a look at black coral; often large pelagics are spotted.

• **Frenchman's Reef**, 10-40 feet. Look for schools of reef fish on this cliff edge boulder. Popular with underwater photographers and beginners.

• **Prickly Pear**, 30-70 feet. An underwater canyon, this site includes ledges, caverns, and is often home of nurse sharks that rest on its sandy bottom.

• **Grouper Bowl**, 25-50 feet. Hard coral formations are found here.

• **The Coliseum**, 25-50 feet. Hard coral formations and schooling fish spotted here.

• **Sand Canyon**, 90 feet. An underwater canyon that comes up to within 25 feet of the surface makes this dive popular.

• **Little Bay** (see photo below), 15-30 feet . Training and night dives often use this site, which is a nursery area for small fish; good underwater photography site.

Seven **wrecks** also lie in the waters off Anguilla. Four were sunk in 1990 as part of an ecological program and all the wrecks are intact and upright on the ocean floor.

Wrecks off Anguilla's shores include:

• **Wreck of Ida Maria**, 60 feet. Deliberately sunk in 1985, this 110-foot freighter is home to many schools of fish and Anguilla's famous lobsters are often spotted here.

• **Wreck of M.V. Sarah**, 80 feet. Deliberately sunk in June, 1990, this 230-foot vessel is home to a wide variety of marine life.

• **Wreck of M.V. Meppel**, 80 feet. Also sink in June 1990, this vessel is intact and sits just inside the sail reef system.

• **Wreck of M.V. Lady Vie**, 80 feet. Another vessel sunk in June 1990, this intact vessel is also located near the sail reef system.

• **Wreck of M.V. Commerce**, 45-80 feet. Sitting on a gently sloping bottom, this 1986 wreck has an abundance of fish life and rays are often spotted here.

Regardless of your swimming abilities, you'll discover that one of Anguilla's best assets is its **beaches**. Miles of shining sand pave the perimeter of this island, which is often cited as one of the top beach destinations in the Caribbean (with good reason). The atmosphere at the various beaches varies from playful to placid. Regardless of which beach you select, the mood is friendly and low-pressure.

Shoal Bay *(see photo below).* Even if you eventually opt for a quieter stretch of sand, budget time for a look at this classic beach, one of the best in the Caribbean. Nearly chalk white sand stretches for two miles and just yards away snorkelers find reefs. Shoal Bay has the most typical "beach bar" atmosphere in Anguilla, with casual eateries and bars sprinkled along the sand. Beach chairs and umbrellas are rented by the day for a few dollars.

SPORTS & RECREATION

Sandy Ground. This beach, stretching alongside the community of Sandy Ground, is a favorite with boaters, windsurfers, water-skiers, and sunbathers. Some of the island's top restaurants are located nearby.

Rendezvous Bay. Largely undeveloped, this beach runs past The Dune Preserve. Take a long stroll on the chalky sand that's occasionally interrupted by rocky shoreline.

Little Bay. This secluded beach is primarily reached by boat and is popular with snorkelers, scuba divers, and birders.

Barnes Bay. Located on the north side of the west end, this beach is popular with snorkelers and windsurfers.

Maundays Bay. Home of Cap Juluca, this half moon crescent invites sunbathing but snorkeling is best enjoyed elsewhere.

BEST SHOPPING

Shopping is not one of Anguilla's strong points. **Artists' galleries** are sprinkled throughout the island, and you'll find the occasional hotel boutique shop.

A good option is an afternoon of shopping on the nearby island of **St. Martin**. Take a ferry ride to Marigot, St. Martin for a few hours at the market or the nearby enclosed **Le West Indies Mall** (primarily fashion and jewelry) or head to the Dutch side's **Philipsburg** for the best selection of duty free items (*see photo below*).

BEST SLEEPS & EATS

Altamer $$$$
This villa complex includes just three ultra-luxury properties; the newest is The African Sapphire. The 14,000-square-foot villa was designed for groups and includes eight bedrooms, home theater, state-of-the-art sound system, flat screen plasma televisions in every room, a private office with high-speed wireless internet access, in-villa fitness center, professional kitchen, multiple hot tubs, and a staff of private butlers. The villa joins two five-bedroom villas at the complex. *Info: Tel. 264/498-4000, www.altamer.com.*

Cap Juluca $$$$
Cap Juluca, named for the native Arawak's Rainbow God, is an exclusive get-away for those looking for privacy and pampering. Fresh from a $22 million renovation, the guest rooms, suites, and vil-  las all offer complimentary mini bar, marble baths, Stearns and Foster beds and Frette linens, 40" Sony Bravia HDTVs and DVD players, Bose Wave stereos with iPod docking stations, and free wireless internet (if you really must). The resort offers tennis (with the services of a resident pro), a 32-foot boat for snorkeling, sunset, and island cruises, a golf aqua driving range, Pilates and yoga classes and more, all located on a spectacular beach on Maundays Bay. *Info: Tel. 888/8JULUCA or 264/497-6666, www.capjuluca.com.*

Cerulean Villa $$$$
Certainly one of Anguilla's most exclusive accommodations is the 13,000-square-foot Cerulean Villa, a favorite with the rich and famous who pay prices of $50,000 a week during high season (and double that during the holidays). During the summer

months, however, the villa is available for more reasonable rates and visitors (14 for the villa) enjoy the seven oceanfront guestrooms, freshwater oceanfront pool, Jacuzzi, tennis courts, tropical gardens, and the meditation and massage garden all set on a magnificent white sand beach. *Info: Tel. 718/522-5358, 264/497-8840, www.cerulean-villa.com.*

Covecastles $$$$

This villa resort caters to the guest looking for privacy, peace, and quiet. These stark white two- and three-bedroom getaways have a contemporary exterior and a tropical decor inside. Complimentary amenities include snorkeling, Sunfish sailboats, sea kayaks, bicycles, tennis, video players and library, concierge service, and a personal housekeeper. Also available at additional charge are deep sea fishing, sailing excursions, tennis instruction, massage, and more. *Info: Tel. 800/223-1108 or 264/497-6801, www.covecastles.com.*

CuisinArt Resort & Spa $$$$

If you cook, you've no doubt heard of CuisinArt. This beachfront resort is owned by the same company. Part of the Leading Small Hotels of the World, this exclusive property is known for its pampering luxury, its fine dining, and its attention to detail. Along with cooking classes, this resort offers its guests tennis, watersports, a beautiful swimming pool, boat charters, mountain biking, scuba diving, a mile-long beach, a full-service spa,

boutique, art gallery, and a variety of cafes and restaurants (featuring produce from the first-ever hydroponic farm at a resort.)

The resort is also home to the new Venus Spa, offering 27,000 square feet of pampering indulgence with 16 treatment rooms, Men's Club Room, VIP suite, an expansive fitness center, relaxation room with sea views, couple's suites and the first aqua therapy pool of its kind in the Caribbean. *Info: Tel. 800/943-3210 or 212/972-0880, 264/498-2000, www.CuisinArtResort.com.*

Kú $$$-$$$$

It's not only its location near the ancient ceremonial site Fountain Cave that gives this resort its name, an Arawak word that means sacred place, but also its relaxing, pampering style. Each of the 27 suites here includes a living/dining room, full kitchen, and a

minimalist style with white furniture and pale aqua walls. The resort is located on Shoal Bay East, which offers excellent diving and snorkeling; other diversions include a large pool, spa, gym, restaurant and bar. *Info: Tel. 800/869-5827 or 264/497-2011, www.ku-anguilla.com.*

Malliouhana Hotel & Spa $$$$

This intimate, 53-room hotel is perched on cliffs overlooking a tranquil sea and yet another example of a perfect Anguillian beach. Guest rooms here are private, spread among 25 mani-cured acres. The resort also includes a pampering spa which features private spa suites with outdoor balconies, an oceanview Jacuzzi, and fitness center. Activities include snorkeling, windsurfing, waterskiing, cruises to nearby cays, windsurfing,

SLEEPS & EATS

Sunfish, Prindle and Hobie catamarans, tennis, and more; deep sea fishing and scuba diving can also be arranged. *Info: Tel. 800/ 835-0796 or 264/497-6111, www.malliouhana.com.*

Blanchards $$$
Since 1994, this dinner-only restaurant has served a sophisticated menu that combines the flavors of the Caribbean, Asia, America and the Mediterranean. Look for dishes including Sesame-Crusted Mahi Mahi with roasted red onions, cherry tomatoes, curried rice, and a sauce made with Dijon mustard and capers or Calypso Chicken, a Caribbean blend of flavors made with ginger, lime and coconut, all pan-roasted and served with creamy polenta and a medley of vegetables. The Blanchards, Bob and Melinda, have authored numerous books including *A Trip to the Beach*, which details their journey to Anguilla. Closed September and October. *Info: Meads Bay, Tel. 264/497-6100, www.blanchardsrestaurant.com.*

The Dune Preserve $-$$
This charming bar and restaurant, set up high above the seashore, is one of the Caribbean's hidden gems. Constructed entirely of recycled ship parts and driftwood, this open-air roost gives visitors the feeling they're visiting Robinson Crusoe. In actuality, they're visiting the restaurant and bar of Bankie Banx, Anguilla's best-known musician. Go for a drink and to enjoy the view, then stay for dinner. besides its title as the island's funkiest bar, this is also one Anguilla's tastiest restaurants (and that's saying something on an island favored by gourmands.) We enjoyed an economical meal of barbecued ribs with rice and peas and a sumptuous seafood salad. Don't miss this one. Open for lunch only, Tuesday through Sunday. *Info: Main Road, no phone, www.bankiebanx.net/Restaurant.html.*

Koalkeel $$$
Now a notable restaurant, Koalkeel was once called The Warden's Place. Built by slaves, many of whom who lived just across the street from the great house, this site originally headed a cotton and sugarcane plantation that spanned the area from The Valley to Crocus Bay. Today the house is furnished with period antiques

SLEEPS & EATS

and includes a 200-year-old oven still used by the restaurant. Enjoy a look at the historic home, visit the upstairs bakery.

The menu includes Island Pea Soup, a puree of pigeon peas and Caribbean sweet potatoes, and Calalloo soup and continues with entrees including coconut shrimp, "Drunken Hen," a Cornish hen baked and blazed with 151 Bacardi, and crayfish grille. The wine list here is a veritable book; the restaurant has its own wine cellar with separate climate controlled rooms for red and white wines. You'll make all the dining decisions at once including dessert selections, made to order. Vanilla crème brulee, mango tarte soufflé and mango sorbet make the perfect end to a meal. Open for dinner only, Monday through Saturday, and complimentary shuttle service is available from Cap Juluca, Malliouhana Hotel, Cuisinart Resort & Spa, Carimar Beach Club, and Anguilla Great House. *Info: The Valley, Tel. 264/497-2930, www.koalkeel.com.*

Pimms Restaurant at Cap Juluca $$$
Fine dining is part of the experience at Cap Juluca's Pimms, which serves up California-Provencal cuisine using local, fresh fish and produce. Specialties include Grilled Peppered Ahi Tuna with Artichoke, Sun Dried Tomato and Olive Vinaigrette, Baby Snapper with Tomato, Black Olive, Fennel and Basil Vinaigrette, and Wild Rice and White Corn Risotto with Grilled Quail. Open for dinner 6:30pm until 10pm, Tuesday through Sunday; closed Monday. *Info: Cap Juluca, Tel. 264/497-6666, www.capjuluca.com/ pimms.php.*

Scilly Cay $$$
This offshore restaurant features Anguillian lobster as well as grilled fish, chicken, and ribs. Just walk up to the dock in Island Harbour and wave and a boat will come over to transport you to

Scilly Cay. Visitors can also enjoy a swim or a snorkel around the reefs. *Info: Island Harbour, Tel. 264/497-5123.*

PRACTICAL MATTERS

Currency. The Eastern Caribbean (EC) currency is legal tender. Value is set at **$1US = 2.68EC**. US dollars are also accepted.

Driving. Driving is English style, on the LEFT.

Electricity. The island has 110 volt electrical currents.

Getting There By Air. Air travelers arrive at Wallblake airport by American Eagle from American's hub in San Juan, Puerto Rico. Another option is the newly-launched Anguilla Air Express with eight-seater flights from San Juan. The emphasis is on first class, personalized service, with an agent meeting all passengers at the gate and escorting them through security and to the departure gate in San Juan, and through Immigration and Customs on arrival in Anguilla, with the same VIP service on the return. Ticket prices are US$399.00 per person, round trip, including taxes. *Info: Tel. 866/966-1881, anguillaairexpress.com.*

Connections are also available from nearby Sint Maarten (either plane or ferry). The flight from Sint Maarten to Anguilla takes approximately 10 minutes. **Winair** offers flights from Sint Maarten's Princess Juliana Airport as well as from Antigua. *Info: Tel. 264/ 497-2748, http://www.fly-winair.com.*

Getting There By Ferry. The 20-30 minute ferry ride from Marigot on the French side of St. Martin to Blowing Point, Anguilla costs US$15 each way (plus a US $3 departure fee each way). The trip takes 20 to 25 minutes.

To take the ferry to Anguilla, stop by the open-air ferry station on the north end of the market in Marigot. Go up to the window, pay your departure tax, and sign up on the manifest sheet, listing your name, passport number, and nationality. You will need your passports for the journey. The ferry fee will be collected on board.

Information. Anguilla Tourist Information Office. *Info: Tel. 877/ 4ANGUILLA (US) or in Anguilla Tel. 264/497-2759.*

Websites. *www.anguilla-vacation.com, charmingescapescollection.com*

PRACTICAL MATTERS

3. ANTIGUA & BARBUDA

Antigua (pronounced an-TEE-ga) doesn't have the quaint shopping zones of islands like St. Martin or the lush tropical beauty of St. Kitts and Nevis.

What Antigua has are beaches: 365 of them, the tourism folks claim. Stretches of white sand that border turquoise waters teeming with marine life. Beaches where you can walk and hardly see another soul. Beaches where you can shop for local crafts and buy a burger at a beachside grill. And beaches where you can just curl up under a tall coconut palm and enjoy the end of another Caribbean day, watching for the green flash as the sun sinks into the sea.

Pre-Colonial Antigua was originally inhabited by the **Siboney Indians**. In 1493 Christopher Columbus named the island in honor of Santa Maria de La Antigua of Seville, a saint at whose namesake church Columbus had prayed before his journey to the Americas.

Antigua has had close ties to England, ever since an English patrol from St. Kitts landed on the island in 1632 and claimed it for the mother country. Since 1981, however, the twin island nation of Antigua and Barbuda has held the status of an independent country.

INTRO

This 108-square mile limestone and coral island is somewhat scrubby with rolling hills, especially on the southern reaches. The capital city is **St. John's**, home of most of the tourist shopping and the cruise port. The south shore of the island is favored by yachties, who call into **Nelson's Dockyard** at **English Harbour**.

North of St. John's lies **Dickenson** and **Runaway Bays**, both popular tourist destinations and known for their excellent beaches. West of St. John's lies **Hawksbill Bay**, home of an excellent resort of the same name with four picturesque beaches.

South of St. John's the roads fan out in various directions around the island. Various routes follow the coastline around **Green Castle Hill**; others take travelers to one of Antigua's top sites: English Harbour. Home of the historic Nelson's Dockyard National Park, this region is a favorite with eco-tourists and history buffs alike.

East of St. John's, roads lead to **Betty's Hope**, an old sugar plantation, and on to the island's most rugged shores. Here the Atlantic waters meet the land, creating beautifully rugged vistas, choppy waters, and several interesting geological formations.

Taxi travel is the most common means of transportation, especially for travelers not comfortable with driving on the left side of the road. Rental cars are available; a temporary Antiguan driver's license is required. The license can be obtained at the **V.C. Bird International Airport** or at any Antiguan police station. We found that some roads are a little bumpy, and that a full tank of gas (as well as a spare tire) was recommended for visitors who would be traveling out on the island away from the major destinations.

BEST SIGHTS IN ANTIGUA

Antigua is also rich in historic attractions as well. The most visited is **Nelson's Dockyard National Park**. Built in 1784, this dockyard was the headquarters for Admiral Horatio Nelson. Today you can retrace the history of this site at the Dow's Hill Interpretation Centre or at the complex's two museums: Admiral's House and Clarence House, former home of Prince William Henry, later known as King William IV of Britain.

St. John's, the capital of Antigua, is the center of both business and tourist activity. Take a stroll around this historic city for a look at **St. John's Cathedral,** perched on a hilltop overlooking town, which was first constructed in 1682 and later replaced in 1789. It was rebuilt and re consecrated in the 19th century after a

devastating earthquake and includes two Baroque style towers.

Also have a walk by **Government House**, the official residence of the Governor General of Antigua, and a good example of 17th century colonial architecture. Also in town, the **Museum of Antigua and Barbuda**, located in the Old Courthouse, includes exhibits of artifacts tracing the history of the islands from prehistoric times through independence.

As a plantation, **Betty's Hope Estate** introduced large-scale sugar cultivation and innovative methods of processing sugar to the island. Founded in the 1650s by Governor Keynell and granted to Christopher Codrington in 1688, the Codrington family had interest in Betty's Hope for more than 250 years until 1920. Both Christopher Codrington and his son served as the Governor General of the Leeward Islands. Today two windmill towers stand along with walls and arches of the boiling house.

BEST FESTIVAL

Sailing is serious business on this island: many call Antigua the sailing capital of the Caribbean. April's annual **Sailing Week** attracts boaters from around the globe to English Harbour Town and is considered one of the world's top regattas. It's certainly **the largest in the Caribbean**, and draws some of the globe's fastest yachts and top crews. Sailing Week isn't all work and no play, however. The week is filled with parties, barbecues, road races, and ends with a grand finale, **Lord Nelson's Ball**.

HOME, SANDY HOME!

With its yacht offerings, fine dining, and year-around good weather, it's no surprise that Antigua has been a home away from home for **many red carpet travelers**. Through the years, Eric Clapton, Oprah Winfrey, Denzel Washington, Giorgio Armani and Morgan Freeman have owned homes here, and stellar sightings are so frequent that *Caribbean Travel and Life* magazine named Antigua the **Best Island for Celebrity Spotting**.

BEST SIGHTS IN BARBUDA

Mention **Barbuda** and most people will recognize the name for one reason: Princess Diana. She and other glitterati sought the seclusion and privacy this island offers.

But Barbuda is more than a jetsetters' hideaway, it's also a nature lovers' island. Accessible as a day trip from Antigua or as a vacation destination of its own, this small island is much less developed than its larger sister. Outside the lavish resorts, the island belongs to the **wildlife**, primarily the feathered variety. It's also noted for its spectacular beaches, long stretches of either pink or white sand that divide the sea from the land.

Along with birders and beach buffs, Barbuda also attracts vacationers looking for quiet fishing, golf, tennis, snorkeling, diving, and beachcombing on its more rugged northeastern Atlantic coast.

SIGHTS

Barbuda is largely unsettled; since Britain established a colony here in 1666, development has been slow. One of the first families was the Codrington's, given a land lease in 1680. The name Codrington remains important in Barbuda today.

Taxis are not just the best way to get around, they're about the only way. Don't look for rental cars on this island. Usually a taxi comes to meet the plane at every landing and can take you anywhere you'd like to go.

Barbuda is well known for its beaches, especially the pink beaches on the southwestern shore. The eastern shore beaches face the Atlantic and the waters here are rougher, but these beaches are best for beachcombing.

Walkers will find some good stretches along this windward

side of the island. The eastern shore is home to the Highlands, steep cliffs that contain many caves, some carved with Amerindian petroglyphs.

Approximately **89 shipwrecks** lie off the Barbuda shore, many of which have not yet been explored. It's an excellent territory for scuba divers as well as snorkelers. However, if you're interested in diving off Barbuda, it is best to make arrangements at a dive shop on Antigua first. These operators can have your dive equipment sent by air or boat to Barbuda.

Birders will find one of the Caribbean's top birding sites on tiny Barbuda. The Frigate Bird Sanctuary, located at the north end of Codrington Lagoon, is only accessible by boat and offers visitors the chance to view these imposing birds. The **frigate bird** (*Fregata Magnificens*) brood their eggs in mangrove bushes along this lagoon. With a seven-foot wingspan, the Frigate Bird or "man o'-war" can fly to 2,000 feet and is avoided by other birds because it often slams into other birds in an attempt to get them to disgorge their food, making an easy meal for the Frigate Bird. The Frigate Bird is easy to spot, especially the male. During mating season, which ranges from September to February, the male inflates a crimson pouch on his throat to try to attract the female. Chicks hatch December to March and remain in the nest for up to eight months.

Other species often spotted include pelicans, warblers, snipes, ibis, herons, kingfishers, tropical mockingbirds, oyster catchers, and cormorants. White-tailed deer, boar, donkeys, and red-footed tortoises are sometimes spotted around the island as well as the famous Barbudian lobster.

Dark Cave is an underground cave with deep pools of clear water that extend approximately one mile under-ground. At **Caves at Two Foot Bay** visitors can climb down into a circular chamber through a hole in the roof to view faded Arawak drawings on the walls. For directions and a local guide, check with your hotel. The **Darby Sink Cave** is another favorite, about 80 feet deep.

Besides animal and bird watching, Barbuda includes several attractions. The ruins of **Martello Tower**, a beachside fortress, is one of the last of its kind in the Caribbean. This former lookout now affords some breathtaking views.

Spanish Point Tower (or The Castle) is another good lookout. Located on the island's southeast side, this tower was originally built to defend the island from the fierce Caribs.

SHOPPING

BEST SHOPPING

The primary shopping area on the island is in St. John's, near the cruise ship terminal. This area doesn't have the charm of many Caribbean shopping districts but it's worth a two- or three-hour excursion to have a look at the goods offered in the small boutiques.

Duty free shopping is the name of the game at nearby **Heritage Quay**; here over 40 shops sell fine jewelry, perfumes, clothing, and more all near the cruise ship terminal. If you'd like to get away from the tourist center, take a walk up to Market Street for shops aimed at the local residents, including many fabric stores offering beautiful tropical prints.

One of St. John's most historic sites is also one of its most popular shopping areas. The waterfront **Redcliffe Quay** has transformed its grim history as a slave-trading block into a bustling shopping and dining destination. Today palates of tropical colors brighten colonial buildings filled with shops selling handicrafts and Caribbean artwork.

When it's time to take a break, grab a local Wadadli beer and sit in the shade of almond trees in the brick courtyards. Outside of St. John's, head to **Harmony Hall** in Brown's Bay Mill. This art gallery, which originated in Jamaica, features work by many Caribbean artists. Original works as well as prints and posters are for sale, accompanied by crafts, books, and seasonings that capture the spice of the island.

BEST SPORTS & RECREATION

Antigua's **beaches**—PR folks like to say there are 365 of them, one for every day of the year—are one of its strongest assets. All beaches are open to the public. Here are some of the best choices for a good beach walk, a day of sunning, or just a little beachcombing:

Dickenson Bay and **Runaway Bay**. Located on the island's northwest side, these resort beaches are developed and offer plenty of fun.

Hawksbill Resort. Located on the northwest side, look for four beaches, the last of which is clothing-optional.

Fort James. Located on the northwest side, this beach is very popular with locals.

Galley Bay. Located on the Northwest Bay, this beach attracts surfers during the winter months when wave action is at a peak.

Rendezvous Bay. Located on the southern coast, this is a quiet beach for those seeking solitude.

Pigeon Point. Located near English Harbour Town, this beach is convenient and a good place to cool off after a day of fun.

Half Moon Bay. Located on the southeast corner of the island, this beach is a national park.

Long Bay. Located on the east side of the island, this beach boasts calm waters protected by a reef and is a good choice for snorkelers and families.

Nature lovers will also find plenty of activity on Antigua. **Scuba diving** and **snorkeling** is a popular activity. Certified divers can enjoy a variety of dives, from walls to wrecks.

SLEEPS & EATS

BEST SLEEPS & EATS

Curtain Bluff $$$$

This exclusive hotel, in operation nearly half a century, is located on a private peninsula with two beaches. The all-inclusive property includes all meals, drinks, afternoon tea, watersports, tennis, golf, and even mail service so you can send those postcards home.

Travelers looking for sports will find a variety of activities to meet their needs at this resort. There are four lighted tennis courts with three full-time tennis pros available, a pro shop with racquet stringing facilities. There is also a squash court, putting green, lawn croquet, and fitness center. You'll find a variety of watersports including scuba diving, deep sea fishing, sailboating, windsurfing and kayaking. For those who just want a little relaxation, there are beach chairs, sun chaises, hammocks and floats. *Info: Tel. 800/ 259-8017 or 268/462-8400, www.curtainbluff.com.*

Hawksbill Antigua by Rex Resorts $$

Located just a few minutes from St. John's, this quiet resort is our favorite kind: quiet, restful, and located on, not one, but four superb beaches. With a primarily British contingency, the resort is somewhat reserved but is just a few minutes from the action of St. John's. Activities at this resort range from relaxing to adventurous. Travelers looking for quiet activities can go out on a paddleboat, play tennis or go shopping at the Hawksbill boutique. More daring visitors can try sailing, waterskiing or snorkeling—or head to the clothing-optional beach, the only one on the island. At the end of the day, enjoy music, limbo dancers or cocktail parties. *Info: Tel. 268/462-0301, www.rexresorts.com.*

The Inn at English Harbor $$$

Fresh from a recent renovation, this colonial-style inn is located on 19 acres near the historic town of English Harbor. Rooms feature dark mahogany wood floors, large modern bathrooms with a separate toilet and bidet, and king-sized beds decorated with Egyptian cotton sheets and pillows while traditional beach cabanas feature Italian Brera marble floors, cane furniture and a verandah that walks directly out to a palm-shaded beach. All accommodations feature flat screen televisions, iPod docking stations and WiFi internet access. *Info: Tel. 268/460-1014, www.theinn.ag.*

K Club $$$$

Located on the sister island of Barbuda, the K Club is one of the Caribbean's most secluded resorts, the spot Princess Diana once went to get away from it all. The resort includes 40 guest rooms on the beach with kitchenettes, gar-

den showers, and air-conditioning. Rates include all meals (but not beverages). The rates are ghastly, even by high Caribbean standards...if you have to ask, you probably can't afford to stay here. A flight on the K Club plane from Antigua adds $400 per person to the cost. *Info: www.kclubbarbuda.com.*

Sandals Grande Antigua Resort & Spa $$$

Like the other couples-only resorts in this popular all-inclusive chain, Sandals Antigua offers an array of activities that can keep even the most restless vacationer happy. Activity coordinators keep things going for those who want to stay busy. For couples preferring inactivity, two-person hammocks and "love baskets," swinging wicker baskets, offer quiet afternoons beneath shady palapas. You'll find a variety of room options here; we stayed in a rondoval; these round cottages include plunge pools. The new, all-suite Mediterranean Village is a popular option. Wherever you stay, you'll enjoy nine restaurants, a beautiful beach, and a full menu of all-inclusive activities. *Info: Tel. 800/SANDALS, www.sandals.com.*

SLEEPS & EATS

St. James Club & Villas $$$$

Like the sand castles built by visiting children on its two powder white beaches, this family-friendly resort is a fantasy retreat  where dreams become reality. In The Village, 41 hillside villas feature all the comforts of home, including a living room, dining room and a full kitchen, while the 147 accommodations at The Club, complete with air-conditioning, cable TV, a safe and a private balcony or terrace, provide easy access to the hub of this Caribbean hideaway. The resort boasts four swimming pools (one adults-only and one for families), six tennis courts, four restaurants, a spa and fitness center. *Info: Tel. 800/345-0356, 954/481-8787, www.stjamesclubantigua.com.*

Sunsail Colonna Club $-$$

If you love the water and sailing, then you'll love Sunsail. This international company, with clubs as far away as Turkey, is a favorite among the sailing set. Here you'll find an array of vessels to take out and enjoy and, if you don't know stern from bow, you can take expert lessons here as well, all part of the all-inclusive plan.

Sunsail isn't fancy but all rooms are air-conditioned and include satellite TV, telephone, mini refrigerator, and tea and coffee making facilities. Choose from twin and double rooms as well as apartments and two- and three-bedroom villas. The resort includes a restaurant, pool, tennis, volleyball, and table tennis as well as a new spa.

But the real attraction here comes in the form of watersports. The resort hugs a small cove where instruction is available in dinghy, catamaran, and yacht sailing as well as waterskiing and windsurfing. If your skills are up to par, you can take a vessel out or participate in one of the resort programs such as a yacht regatta or dinghy regatta. Waters are their most challenging during the winter months but summer usually brings milder trade winds and conditions better suited to beginners. *Info: Tel. 866/786-7370, www.sunsail.com.*

Admiral's Inn $$-$$$
This inn is home to a very popular eatery with outdoor dining near the yachts that come to this dockyard from around the Caribbean. Along with great people-watching, the restaurant also offers breakfast, lunch, and dinner. Save time before dinner for a stop by the lounge area filled with yacht club flags. *Info: Nelson's Dockyard, Tel. 268/460-1027.*

Chez Pascal $$$
Dine in the dining room or the garden at this fine restaurant located at Cross and Tanner Streets. *Info: Galley Bay, Five Island, Tel. 268/462-3232.*

THE SKINNY ON ANTIGUAN EATS

Although Antigua boasts numerous high-end international restaurants, for many diners home-style cooking remains tops. Dishes for years featured in local homes for Sunday dinner are now often spotted on some island menus, offering the chance to try Antigua's own distinct combination of Creole recipes with English influences.

The national dish of Antigua is **fungi and pepperpot**, a thick stew made with a medley of vegetables including yam, okra, plantain, pumpkin, and more with salted meat, accompanied by fungi (pronounced foon-jee), a cornmeal dish. Another flavorful soup— one you'll find everywhere from local restaurants to street stands—is **goat water**. This goat soup is seasoned with peppers as well as cloves and cinnamon.

A local favorite sweet is **ducana**, a pudding made from grated sweet potato and coconut, sugar and spices, all boiled while wrapped in a banana leaf. And save room to finish off your meal with a taste of the extra-sweet Antigua **black pineapple**.

SLEEPS & EATS

Hemingway's Caribbean Cafe $-$$

Located near Heritage Quay, this informal, second story restaurant is located in a West Indian-styled building constructed in the early 1800s. Start with a Hemingway's fruit punch or pineapple daiquiri then move on to an entree of Caribbean seafood or steak. *Info: St. Mary's Street, Tel. 268/462-2763.*

Le Bistro $$$

The island's first French restaurant, this eatery is known for its haute cuisine and includes local dishes such as medallions of fresh local lobster in basil, white wine and brandy sauce. Open for dinner only, Tuesday-Sunday. Call for reservations. *Info: Hodges Bay, Tel. 268/462-3881.*

Lookout Restaurant $-$$
With views of Nelson's Dockyard, this restaurant serves up local specialties: spiny lobster soup, codfish balls, Antiguan pineapple and grilled lobster with lime butter. Steel bands entertain on Sunday afternoons. *Info: Shirley Heights, Tel. 268/ 460-1785.*

PRACTICAL MATTERS

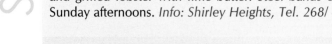

Currency. The Eastern Caribbean (EC) dollar is the legal tender. It is exchanged at a fixed rate of $1 US = 2.68EC. American dollars are also accepted.

Driving. Driving is on the LEFT.

Getting There. Most travelers enter the island at V.C. Bird International Airport, located on the island's north-northeast coast (15-20 minutes from St. John's).

Information. Department of Tourism, *Tel. 212/541-4117 or 888/268-4227.*

Website. *www.antigua-barbuda.org*

PRACTICAL MATTERS

4. ARUBA

Aruba has its own special beauty. Don't look for mountains covered with tall palms. Or walkways lined with flowering bougainvillea. Or roads shaded by willowy casuarina trees.

Instead, you'll have to search a little deeper for the beauty of Aruba. You'll have to venture to the rugged Atlantic shore and watch the tumultuous waves carving the rocky shore, continually changing the demarcation line where the land meets the sea. Or you can hike to some of Aruba's highest hills, curious bumps on the landscape, and look out at the *cunucu* or countryside for traditional Dutch-style houses with their sun-baked orange tile roofs.

INTRO

The best way to see the beauty of Aruba is to look into the faces of the Aruban people, the island's greatest asset. This tiny island, a mere 70 square miles, truly is a melting pot of cultures. Over **43 nationalities** are represented here, and with them a mélange of languages. Arubans learn from an early age the benefits and necessity of working with other nations and learning different languages is a skill that most young Arubans master. The language of the Aruban home is **Papiamento**, a mixture of Spanish, Portuguese, French, Dutch, Indian, English, and even some African dialects. When youngsters head to school, they receive instruction in **Dutch**, because of Aruba's continuing ties to the Kingdom of Holland. Once they reach third or fourth grade, instruction in **English** begins. **Spanish** is introduced during the junior high years, and in high school students select from **French** or **German**.

That familiarity with many languages translates into a welcoming atmosphere for visitors of any nationality. There is no language barrier to overcome. There is just a spirit of "Bon Bini" or "Welcome" which greets visitors from the moment they arrive in the airport and continues throughout their visit.

Taxis are available in resort areas or you can have one dispatched by calling 22116 or 21604 on island. Rates are fixed (no meters), so check with your driver before the ride. Rental cars are commonplace and a good option if you'd like to do a lot of exploration.

BEST SIGHTS IN ARUBA

Although the beaches are tempting, be sure to have a look at the rest of the island. The biggest tour operator is **DePalm Tours** (*Tel. 297-582-4400, www.depalm.com*), with desks in every major hotel. This firm offers an excellent half-day tour aboard air-conditioned motor coaches with hotel pick-up. At the conclusion of the tour, you can return to your hotel or get off in downtown Oranjestad for an afternoon of shopping. One of the most popular tour options are the **open-air jeep safaris** of the island's rugged countryside; hop aboard an open-air, yellow jeep and bounce along the desert terrain for the best view of this unique island.

For an excellent view of the *cunucu*, or countryside, stop at the **Casibari Rock Forma-**
tion. It's a fairly easy climb (although you'll find yourself bent over and squeezing between rocks a few times), but wear good shoes for this trek.

For all of Aruba's attractions, many visitors, especially those staying a week or longer, opt for a **day trip** off the island. Although day trips to Venezuela's Angel Falls were formerly popular, today the top day trip is **Curaçao**. After a half hour flight aboard Dutch Antilles Express (*Tel. 011/599-717-0808, www.flydae.com*), travelers reach the large Dutch island. Curaçao's capital of **Willemstad** is by Caribbean standards a major metropolitan area with a harbor consistently rated about the fifth busiest in the world. This truly international city boasts streets lined with Dutch-style architecture as colorful as a

candy store. Beyond Willemstad, Curaçao becomes a countryside dotted with tall cacti trimmed with coastlines of the windswept and tranquil varieties. Natural attractions like **Hato Caves** and **Christoffel National Park** draw many day trippers.

BEST SHOPPING

Aruba definitely ranks as a top Caribbean shopping destination. International goods — perfumes, china, crystal, jewelry, cameras, and clothing— are best buys. Unlike the practice of many islands, bargaining is not customary in Aruba.

Stores are open 8am to 6:30pm, Monday through Saturday, and usually close for two hours during lunch. If a cruise ship is in port, you may find some shops open on Sunday.

The primary shopping district stretches **along Oranjestad's waterfront**. Malls as colorful as sherbet line this route, tempting shoppers with goods that range from T-shirts and Delft Blue salt and pepper shakers to European *tres chic* designer outfits and fine jewelry.

Seaport Mall and **Seaport Marketplace** have the lion's share of the mall business. The Mall is located adjacent to Renaissance Resort and includes high-priced shops on its lowest level. Upstairs, boutiques offer moderately priced resort wear, jewelry, china, and more for a total of over 65 shops.

If you forget someone special on your list, you'll also find shops at the Queen Beatrix International Airport.

BEST SPORTS & RECREATION

Kicking back in Aruba largely centers around kicking up a little surf. On the southwest end of the island, **Palm** and **Eagle beaches** are some of the most popular because of their proximity to the major hotels, but for the calmest waters head to Baby Beach. Located on the far southern tip of the island near the town of San Nicolas, it is well-known for its lake-calm waters. Swimmers should avoid the waters of the island's north shore, which are rough and often plagued by undertow.

Divers will find numerous **dive sites** in the 40- to 60-foot depth range, including the *Antilla*, a German freighter that's the largest wreck in the Caribbean, and the wreck of the *California*, the ship that didn't respond to the distress signals of the *Titanic*.

Above the waves, Aruba offers some of the Caribbean's top **windsurfing**. Fisherman's Hut is an ideal beginner's site because of its calm, shallow waters, while experts head for Boca Grandi's rough waves. Every year, the island hosts the Aruba Hi-Winds Pro

BEST FESTIVAL
Scheduled for the days surrounding Memorial Day in the US, the **Aruba Soul Beach Music Festival** is a star-studded affair held on **Havana Beach**. Along with soul tunes, look for R&B as well as special comedy nights. Past performers have included Sean Paul, Chaka Khan, Wyclef Jean, Lauryn Hill, Nina Sky, Anthony Hamilton, Alicia Keys and Brian McKnight.

Am World Cup featuring the best competitors from the world of windsurfing.

Aruba also has a championship **golf course**. Tierra Del Sol (*www.tierradelsol.com*), designed by Robert Trent Jones II, combines sand dunes, cacti, rock formations, and views of the sea.

Guided **horseback rides** at Rancho Del Campo (*www.ranchodelcampo.com*) are popular with many travelers. On tours, you can ride through Aruba's only national park: Arikok National Wildlife Park, home of Indian rock markings, gold digging ruins, and a restored *cunucu* home.

SPORTS & RECREATION

BEST SLEEPS & EATS

Aruba Marriott Resort & Stellaris Casino $$$$

Located on Palm Beach, the 411-room Aruba Marriott Resort & Stellaris Casino has undergone a recent renovation and now

sports a fresh new look throughout, from guest rooms, to the 6,500-square-foot spa, to the largest casino in Aruba. One of the newest features of the hotel is the Tradewinds Club, an upscale, 59-room "hotel within a hotel" located on the top floor of the resort and providing personalized service and privileges including access to a private 1900-square-foot lounge area with a terrace. *Info: Tel. 800/223-6388, 297-586-9000, www.marriott.com.*

Hyatt Regency Aruba Resort & Casino $$$$

Located on Palm Beach, the Hyatt Regency Aruba Resort & Casino is one of Aruba's most luxurious properties. The recently renovated resort is for anyone looking for a body holiday. Be pampered in the health and fitness facility, slice across the clear Caribbean on a sailboat at the watersports facility, or just luxuriate in the warmth of the sun at the three-level pool complex. The

resort's 360 guest rooms and suites include 32" LCD TVs, high-speed Internet access, and Hyatt's signature Grand Beds. The hotel's Copacabana Casino offers over 260 slot machines and 21 gaming tables and

"Carnival in Rio" most nights with live music and dancing. *Info: Tel. 800/233-1234, 297-586-1234, aruba.hyatt.com.*

Occidental Grand Aruba $$$-$$$$
Located on Palm Beach, this all-inclusive, 398-guest room retreat (formerly the Allegro Aruba Grand Resort) offers an on-site casino, six restaurants featuring global gastronomic delights, a spa and salon. Get busy with diving lessons with PADI-certified instructors, or enjoy sailing, snorkeling or kayaking excursions. Landlubbers can also head to the tennis courts. *Info: Tel. 800/ 858-2258, www.occidentalhotels.com.*

Radisson Aruba Resort, Casino & Spa $$$-$$$$
Located on Palm Beach, this 354-room hotel has plenty to keep vacationers busy on the beach with water-skiing, wave runners, catamarans, kay-aks, canoes and scuba instruction. The hotel boasts a 1500-foot-wide stretch of sand and two zero-entry free form pools. Guest rooms are deco-rated in Colonial West Indian fur-nishings including four-poster beds and balconies with teak furniture. The resort is home to four restaurants and lounges, a new 13,000-square-foot Larimar Spa, and casino. *Info: Tel. 800/ 395-7046 or 297-586-6555, www.radisson.com/aruba.*

Renaissance Aruba Resort & Casino $$$-$$$$
This resort offers two distinct options: the Renaissance Marina Hotel (on the land side and popular for adults who want to be closer to the nightlife) or the Renaissance Ocean Suites, the best family choice thanks to its oceanside location and all-suites offerings. In the Ocean Suites, the renovated guest rooms include a king bed, a living room with a queen sofa bed, minibar, fridge, coffeemaker, high-speed internet access (there is a surcharge for

SLEEPS & EATS

access), and either a balcony or patio. One of the real highlights of this property is the 40-acre private Renaissance Island, home to Aruba's only private beaches. You'll find dining on Renaissance Island as well as at the hotels; numerous restaurants and bars range from a steakhouse to an adults-only martini bar. *Info: Tel. 800/421-8188 or 297-583-6000, www.marriott.com.*

Charlie's Bar $$-$$$

Located in San Nicolas, about a 15-minute drive from downtown Oranjestad, lies Aruba's best known and loved bar. Since 1941, Charlie's has served drinks to generations of local residents and Caribbean travelers looking for a watering hole. Many of those visitors have left memorabilia—from yacht flags to pieces of clothing—on every available surface in the structure. After a drink, settle in for a lunch or dinner of garlic shrimp, beef tenderloin, surf and turf, fresh fish, or just a burger. The restaurant also offers wireless internet access. *Info: Mainstreet, San Nicolas, Tel. 297-584-5086.*

ARUBAN CUISINE

As you would expect on an island that's home to 40 nationalities, Aruba offers cuisine from around the globe. Chinese, Indonesian, French, Japanese, Argentinean, Italian, Russian, Spanish, Mediterranean, Dutch, and American food are found around the island. But don't miss the Aruban dishes. Fried fish with funchi (cornmeal), stewed lamb with *pan bati* (pancake), and *keshi yena* (a hollowed wheel of Edam cheese filled with meat and baked to combine flavors) are popular local dishes.

La Trattoria El Faro Blanco $$$$

Located in the building that once served as home to the keeper of the California Lighthouse, one of Aruba's most photographed sites, this building offers indoor and outdoor dining and is a favorite with romantics. Italian cuisine is the specialty of the house; dishes including beef tenderloin Carpaccio, Risotto Lobster and Osobucco draw many repeat visitors. Reservations are recommended, especially for sunset dining. *Info: California Lighthouse Tel. 297-586-0786, www.aruba-latrattoria.com.*

The Old Cunucu House Restaurant $$$$
Housed in a restored 150-year-old Aruban homestead within walking distance of the resorts of Palm Beach, this well-known restaurant features local cuisine. The restaurant offers specialties such as Aruban fish soup, *keshi yena*, fresh conch, or seafood Palm Beach, a dish of lobster, fish, scallops, and squid with a cream sauce with wine and flamed with pernod. Other dishes such as Cornish hen, New York sirloin, and coconut fried shrimp are also available. Open for lunch and dinner Monday through Saturday. Reservations are recommended. *Info: Palm Beach 150, Tel. 011/297-586-1666, www.theoldcunucuhouse.com.*

PRACTICAL MATTERS

Currency. The Aruban florin or Aruban guilder is the official currency but US dollars are also widely accepted. At press time the exchange rate was $1US to A.Fl. 1.79 although this fluctuates.

Driving. Driving is on the right side of the road.

Electricity. North American appliances may be used without adapters. Voltage is 110 volts, 60 cycles.

Getting There. Aruba is a 2-1/2 hour flight from Miami or four hours from New York. Direct service into the expanded Queen Beatrix International Airport is available from major US and Canadian carriers. The airport offers US Customs preclearance, a real timesaver for American travelers headed home.

Information. *Tel. 800/TO-ARUBA*

Website. *www.aruba.com*

PRACTICAL MATTERS

5. BARBADOS

George Washington slept here.

Really. The tiny island of **Barbados** has been welcoming tourists since the days before the American Revolution. George himself came to enjoy the healthful climate (much needed by his tuberculosis-stricken brother, Lawrence) back in 1751, and visitors have been coming to this island in the far eastern Caribbean ever since.

The reasons are easy to see. An idyllic climate. An atmosphere that combines tropical casualness with British formality, where high tea on a hot afternoon makes perfect sense. A history that includes not only presidents but pirates, and great houses that recall the days of vast plantations and a jungle of sugar cane.

INTRO

Today **Barbados** exudes the most British atmosphere found in the Caribbean. As you drive through the island, look for both men and women in cool white suits on the cricket fields. In the afternoons, take time to enjoy high tea. And listen to the voices of the Barbadians or Bajans (rhymes with Cajun): their accent is almost British.

Barbados is a pear-shaped island with gentle rolling hills. Agriculture still rules much of the landscape, and **cane** is still king. Although sugar prices have dropped severely in recent years, the crop is a Barbadian mainstay. A drive through the island will take you through miles of cane, often with nothing but the road before and behind you visible during the peak of the growing season.

The **most easterly of the Caribbean islands**, Barbados has strongly differentiated east and west sides. On the Atlantic side, currents are strong, and jagged cliffs and sea caves are carved by the water's force. In contrast, western beaches offer placid Caribbean waters with excellent visibility, little current, and a gentle trade breeze.

Taxis are prevalent but not inexpensive. Rental cars are available; a Barbados drivers license is required. Many visitors rent **"Mini-Mokes,"** a cross between a jeep and a dune buggy. And, don't forget, driving is on the left side of the road.

SIGHTS

BEST SIGHTS IN BARBADOS

Enjoy a ride into **Harrison's Cave**, where damp rooms reveal their hidden formations, waterfalls, and pools and is especially known for its extensive stalactite and stalagmite formations. Barbados's top visitor attraction now features six new trams including two wheelchair-accessible trams. A new Cave Interpretive Center features multimedia presentations.

A sea cave rather than a cavern, the **Animal Flower Cave** is named for the sea anemones found in its pools. Located on one of Barbados's most northern points, the cave is reached after a hike down steep steps carved into the coral cliffside. Halfway down, the roar of the sea greets visitors as dark blue breakers (which are teeming with sharks) churn just outside, occasionally spraying into the cool stony recesses. The sea waves long ago carved this cave from the coral which underlies much of Barbados. Like an aquatic bulldozer, the pounding waves have chipped away at the rocky precipice and left this multiroom sea cave.

In the heart of the island lies the **Barbados Wildlife Reserve**, a sprawling forest that's best known as home of the Barbados **Green Monkey**.

Brought by early settlers to the island, today the monkeys run rampant, often cursed by farmers for stealing mangoes or bananas. The monkeys are best spotted in the mornings and evenings; they spend their afternoons at nearby Grenade Hall Forest, a former dump that has been given a new life as a protected

SIGHTS

biome and trail. During the cooler hours, however, the monkeys can be spotted at the Wildlife Reserve, scampering among four acres of mahogany trees.

Monkeys are also often spotted at **Welshman Hall Gully**, a ravine filled with over 200 varieties of tropical plants. A mile-long walk down an avenue of graceful palms leads to a jungle walk through clove, nutmeg, fig, and other species. A canopy of verdant growth shades the walk through much of the gully, which was named for the Welshman who first settled this valley formed by a crack in the coral limestone. His descendants later cleared part of the forest to cultivate fruit trees but later the land was allowed to return to its natural state.

BEST FESTIVAL

Traditionally celebrated at the end of the sugar cane season, **Crop Over Festival** has become a month-long party spanning July. This island-wide celebration includes weeks of competitions and festivities that exhibit Barbadian arts, foods, music, and dance. The fun begins with the ceremonial delivery of the Last Canes. **Calypso** is the music of this festival and fills the air at concerts and road marches, all culminating in a carnival parade called the **Grand Kadooment**.

BEST SHOPPING

Bridgetown along **Broad Street** is the main shopping area. Here you'll shop for fine goods of every variety: luggage, designer clothing, china, crystal, silver, cameras, the list goes on. Barbados is a tax-free haven, so you'll enjoy savings. Only liquor must be delivered to the airport or the cruise port; other purchases can be carried out from the store.

In Bridgetown, the **Cave Shepherd Shop** offers china, crystal, fine clothing, electronics, and perfumes. Located on Broad Street, this shop has been serving Barbados visitors and residents since 1906. Today it includes a Columbian Emeralds International outlet with fine jewelry as well as restaurants, an activities desk for island tours, photo lab, and more. Other Bridgetown shopping malls include **Sunset Mall** and **DaCostas Mall**, with shops offering everything from perfumes to china to cameras. For island crafts, drop by the **Medford Craft Village** in **St. Michael**. Hand-carved items such as birds, boats, clocks, and fish are made here from local mahogany.

BEST SPORTS & RECREATION

Barbados is home to many **beaches** where travelers can

snorkel in calm Caribbean waters or enjoy windswept vistas on the Atlantic shoreline. Swimmers should head to the Caribbean coast; precautions should be taken not to get over waist deep in the often-dangerous Atlantic currents, which are preferred by windsurfers and sailors.

Swimmers are better off with the calm waters found on **Mullins Beach**, **Crane Beach**, and **Dover Beach**.

The center of activity in the central region of Barbados is the coastal town of **Bathsheba**, tucked at the base of the hills. For many travelers, part of the allure of Bathsheba is its tumultuous Atlantic waters, perfect for **surfing**. Here huge boulders, like a giant's beach toys, litter the sand. Beyond the water's edge, the sea breaks into rows of pounding surf, especially at a spot deemed **"the Soup Bowl."**

BEST SLEEPS & EATS

Almond Beach Club & Spa $$-$$$

This adults-only all-inclusive resort is restricted to guests age 16 and over, promising a quiet, relaxed stay. Located on the west coast of Barbados, Almond Beach Club offers 161 rooms along with three pools, sailboats, snorkeling gear, windsurfing equipment, pedal boats, kayaks, water skis, banana boats, rods and reels for fishing off the beach, and one lighted tennis court. The

spa, priced a la carte, provides treatments ranging from Thalassotherapy algae and seaweed baths to couples massages and aromatherapy salt scrubs. *Info: Tel. 800/4ALMOND, 246/432-7840, www.almondresorts.com.*

SLEEPS & EATS

Cobblers Cove $$$$

Styled like an English country house, this luxurious resort is a member of Relais & Châteaux. The resort's 40 suites each offer

a living area, balcony or patio, air-conditioned bedrooms, and wet bar with a refrigerator stocked with drinks. Featuring a white powder beach that leads to cobalt blue waters, patrons can explore the ocean either above the waves on kayaks, waterskis or windsails, or below by skimming the surface with snorkels or delving deeper with scuba gear. For a freshwater dip, guests can swim in the hotel pool, while sports enthusiasts can try out a floodlit tennis court, the Keep Fit Centre, complete with sports art bikes and treadmills, or arrange for a round of golf on one of three courses at nearby Sandy Lane. Children aren't permitted from early January through March to keep high season as peaceful and relaxing as possible. *Info: Tel. 800/890-6060, 246/422-2291, www.cobblerscove.com.*

Fairmont Royal Pavilion $$$$

This elegant property is designed for guests looking for the finest

money can buy: from a grand entrance lined with the top-flight boutiques such as Cartier, to the 72 junior suites that overlook the sea. In your room, you'll be pampered as well with twice-daily maid service, a private terrace or patio, and a decor that combines elegance and tropical splendor. Guests also enjoy golf privileges at the Robert Trent Jones, Jr.-designed course, the Royal Westmoreland. Children are welcome at Royal

Pavilion from April through October. *Info: Tel. 866/540-4485, 246/422-5555, www.fairmont.com/royalpavilion.*

Hilton Barbados $$$
This 350-room hotel is just 15 minutes from the airport, a real bonus for travelers after a long flight. Two beaches, a large pool complex, three tennis courts and other diversions offer plenty of activity. *Info: Tel. 877/GO-HILTON, 246/426-0200, www.hiltoncaribbean.com.*

Sandy Lane $$$$
Welcoming some of the world's most elite travelers since 1961, the elegant Sandy Lane recently underwent an extensive refurbishment project. Guests have their choice among 112 rooms and suites as well as a five-bedroom villa, all with Italian marble floors and plantation-style  furniture. Golfers can choose from Sandy Lane's three courses; the most famous is the Tom Fazio-course, the Green Monkey. Relaxation is found in the spa, housed in a Romanesque-style building; treatments blend techniques from the Caribbean, Asia and Europe. *Info: Tel. 246/444-2000, www.sandylane.com.*

BARBADOS CUISINE

Like the variety which spices up the island itself, dining in Barbados can mean everything from beach bars to five stars. Along with traditional Caribbean cuisine, we found that Barbados has some unique dishes of its own. Bajan food includes dishes with such melodious names as **cou-cou** (a cornmeal and okra entree) and **jug-jug** (Guinea corn and green peas) as well as **flying fish** and a spicy stew called **pepperpot**. The most popular drinks are **Banks beer** and **Mount Gay Rum**, both local products.

The Cliff $$$$

A view of the sea complements the bounty of the menu at this West Coast restaurant featuring fish, steaks, and pastas. Look for entrees including chargrilled tuna on garlic mashed potatoes, seared tuna nori, chargrilled barracuda with sweet pepper coulis, and Cajun-styled salmon on Asian noodles. *Info: Derricks, Tel. 246/432-1922, www.thecliffbarbados.com.*

L'acajou $$$$

The signature restaurant of Sandy Lane, this elegant restaurant features entrees ranging from Olive Oil Braised Filet of Turbot to Peppered Loin of Milk Fed Veal. The restaurant also features a wine pairing menu. *Info: Sandy Lane, Tel. 246/444-2000, www.sandylane.com.*

Olives Bar and Bistro $$

This casually elegant eatery offers indoor and courtyard dining in a two-story Barbadian structure. Choose from entrees that range from potato rosti with smoked salmon and sour cream, to Jamaican jerk pork to gourmet pizza. Follow it all up with an espresso at the upstairs bar. *Info: Holetown, Tel. 246/432-2112.*

Ragamuffins Bar & Restaurant $$

West Indian and European cuisine highlight the menu of this restaurant and bar which has been recommended by many US gourmet publications. Look for dishes including Blackened Fish /w Garlic Aioli, Caribbean Stir Fry Shrimp, West Indian Curry, and more including a wine menu. *Info: First Street, Holetown, Tel. 246/432-1295, ragamuffinsbarbados.com.*

PRACTICAL MATTERS

Currency. The Barbados dollar (BDS) is the official currency. The Barbados dollar converts at 1.98BDS = $1US. The rate does not fluctuate but is fixed to the US dollar. Both US and Canadian dollars are widely accepted.

Electricity. 115 volts/50 cycles

Getting There. The Grantley Adams International Airport is served by major US and Canadian carriers. Flying time from New York to Barbados is about four and half hours.

Information. Barbados Tourism Authority, *Tel. 866/566-0956*

Website. *www.visitbarbados.org*

6. BRITISH VIRGIN ISLANDS

Hoist the sails and gather way. Grip the wheel in your hands and cut a feather through aquamarine waters to a quiet Caribbean cove. Drop anchor and motor a small launch to an empty beach for a gourmet picnic lunch on white sand.

Sound like a boating fantasy? It is, but in the **British Virgin Islands** (BVI), it is also reality. Year around, skippers and would-be boaters come from around the world to sail these calm waters and take advantage of a group of 50 islands that call themselves "Nature's Little Secrets." Unlike their nearby American cousins, these Virgin Islands are not a shopper's paradise, but one for nature lovers looking for quiet getaways, empty beaches, and a maritime atmosphere.

INTRO

Boats of every description come to this capital of the Caribbean boating world. But long before today's sleek vessels made the BVI a popular port of call, Christopher Columbus plied these waters. The explorer landed on the island of Tortola in 1694. The multitude of surrounding tiny islands reminded Columbus of the tale of Saint Ursula and her 11,000 virgins so he named these the Virgin Islands.

Although there are over 50 islands in the chain, only a handful have facilities for travelers. **Tortola**, named for the turtle doves found here, is the largest island with only 21 square miles. Don't let distance fool you, however. Because of steep hills, a car trip around or across the island is a slow undertaking.

One of the best ways to see Tortola, and all the British Virgin Islands, is by boat. Even if you don't know rigging from rudder, you can enjoy a vacation at sea thanks to skippered boat programs. For about the same cost as a stay at a luxury resort, you can enjoy a week aboard a vessel with a skipper to man the wheel and a cook to prepare local dishes like fried conch or rice and peas.

Tortola's largest community, **Road Town**, is the home office of the largest charter yacht company in the world. Visit The Moorings to view the huge fleet of yachts managed by the company and owned by sailors around the globe.

Set your course for **Jost Van Dyke**, an island named for a Dutch pirate. Jost (pronounced Yost) Van Dyke is a real getaway, a Robinson Crusoe kind of place without luxury hotels, gourmet restaurants or pricey shops. What Jost Van Dyke does have are nearly deserted beaches, coral reefs teeming with colorful fish, and a place called Foxy's.

Foxy's Tamarind Bar is a landmark in the world of Caribbean boaters. It is located beneath palm thatched roofs plastered with boat flags, skippers hats, and business cards left here by visitors. The restaurant serves West Indian specialties like curried chicken *rotis*, but the real

treat is Foxy himself. Foxy, a.k.a. Philicianno Callwood, is a one-man show greeting incoming guests with impromptu songs sung to a calypso beat.

Jost Van Dyke may be named for a pirate, but the best known pirate connections in the BVI are **Norman Island** and **Dead Chest**. Norman Island is thought to have been the inspiration for Robert Lewis Stevenson's *Treasure Island*. Dead Chest is the island where the pirate Blackbeard allegedly marooned 15 men and one bottle of rum, starting a fight that left no survivors. The incident inspired the mariners' ditty: "Fifteen men on a dead man's chest. Yo ho ho and a bottle of rum."

A popular port of call is **Virgin Gorda** (the fat virgin), the second largest island in the BVI. **The Baths**, Virgin Gorda's most photographed attraction *(see photos on page 58 and 61)*, can be reached by land or sea. Left by volcanic upheaval, The Baths are formed by giant boulders that provide a picturesque contrast to the white beach. Duck between boulders to enter the sea cave where you can wade in the cool, shady baths.

Although some hotels feature local musicians, don't look for casinos or nightclubs in these Caribbean islands. The BVI makes no claim to being a swinging destination, and even in the large resorts most activity stops by 11pm.

The reason is simple. Only hours away, the sun will again rise on another Caribbean day. And across the British Virgin Islands, boaters want to be ready.

Getting around the BVI can involve a combination of car and boat travel, depending on if you'll be doing some island hopping. Taxis are an easy way to get around any of the islands. Rental cars can be obtained on Tortola, Virgin Gorda and Anegada. You'll need to obtain a temporary BVI driving license for US$10; you'll need to show the car rental agency your valid drivers license from home and you must be at least 25 years old. Driving is on the left side of the road.

A network of inter-island ferries connect the islands of the BVI. For a list of the numerous ferry companies and their ferry ports, visit www.bvitourism.com.

🚶 BEST SIGHTS IN THE BVI

One top destination in the BVI (or, for that matter, in the Caribbean) is **The Baths**. This 682-acre park is located on Virgin Gorda, and it's so unique that once you visit it you'll be able to spot this park in any Caribbean video or magazine. Unlike most Caribbean beaches which are mostly flat, this site is scattered with massive granite boulders. As smooth as riverbed stones, these gargantuan rocks litter the sea and the beach. They also form shadowy caves where you can swim in water that's lit by sunlight filtering through the cracks. This unique site is un-

spoiled and a fun snorkeling spot as well.

Getting out on the water—whether that means sailing, windsurfing, kayaking, parasailing, surfing, or powerboating—is the top activity throughout these islands. The British Virgin Islands Tourist Board's official website (see below) has a full list of outfitters that can set you up, whether you're an expert or wanting to learn a new watersport.

Hikers should save time for a visit to **Sage Mountain National Park** on Tortola. The BVI's highest point has an altitude of 1,780 feet and is lush with greenery that can be viewed from its many gravel walkways.

SHOPPING

BEST SHOPPING

Unlike the "other" Virgin islands, shopping is not a major attraction of the BVI. However, you will find a good variety of shops in **Road Town** and **West End** at **Soper's Hole**. Spices are popular buys, from hot sauces to West Indian mustards to chutney. One of the best selections is found at **Sunny Caribbee**, *Main Street, Road Town, Tel. 284/494-2178*. It has a good collection of things Caribbean, including local crafts, cookbooks, and art prints.

For inexpensive buys, visit the open-air market on Main Street. Here you can haggle for jewelry, T-shirts, calabash bags, and straw hats. The mood is friendly, and you'll be entertained most days by steel band musicians.

BEST SPORTS & RECREATION

Want to swim with dolphins? Check out **Dolphin Discovery**, *Tel. 866/393-5158 in US, 866-793-1905 in Canada, www.dolphindiscovery.com.*

This outfitter offers several dolphin programs for different activity and budget levels ranging from encounters on a waist-deep platform to swims that allow you to be pushed by the feet by two dolphins and more.

SPORTS & RECREATION

BEST FESTIVAL

Not surprisingly, many BVI special events are boat races. One of the biggest is the **BVI Spring Regatta and Sailing Festival** in early April. Sailors from around the globe come to compete in this yachting event.

BEST SLEEPS & EATS

Biras Creek Resort $$$$
Virgin Gorda's Biras Creek makes a mighty tempting offer to lovers: they'll maroon you on a deserted beach for the day. Just the two of you, a picnic basket and paradise. Problem is, it's pretty tough to leave Biras Creek itself. This luxurious resort on Deep Bay combines beach resort and yacht club.

Tucked on the north end of Virgin Gorda on a 140-acre peninsula, this 31-suite resort is a favorite with travelers looking for a relaxing getaway at the private beach, walking on nearby nature trails, and exploring the island. Each suite includes bicycles; you'll also enjoy use of two tennis courts, and complimentary use of snorkels, fins, windsurfers, sailboats, and motor dinghies, including free instruction. The resort is also home to a pampering spa; its signature treatment is the Island Cooler, which incorporates an invigorating salt scrub, freshly picked aloe, and a soothing body wrap and massage. *Info: Tel. 877/883-0756 or 284/494-3555, www.biras.com.*

Bitter End Yacht Club & Resort $$$$
This resort is located at the "bitter end" of the BVI on the North Sound. Reached only by boat, this resort gives you the feeling of staying at a yacht club, where days are spent in close connection with the sea. The resort boasts the largest fleet of recreational boats in the

SLEEPS & EATS

Caribbean. Many guests arrive via their own craft and simply dock for their stay. Those without a boat can stay in a resort room or aboard one of the club yachts. Spend the day in your "room" boating among the islands, then return to port at night and enjoy a quiet meal in the resort's elegant restaurant.

Other activities at the resort include guided nature hikes or striking out on your own on the hiking trails, and cruises to the Baths and Anegada in the BVI. Travelers can also take out a Boston Whaler skiff to a nearby private island for a quiet picnic. You can also pamper yourself with a visit to the spa, which utilizes locally-grown plants including neem, aloe vera, and coconut in its treatments. *Info: Tel. 800/872-2392 or 284/494-2746, www.beyc.com.*

Long Bay Beach Resort & Villas Tortola $$$

They call this resort Long Bay but we found that they might as well change the name to Long Beach. A mile-long white sand beach is the central focal point of this 105-room resort located near Tortola's West End. All rooms, both hilltop and beachside, have views of the beach and the quiet waters of Long Bay. The resort includes a spa and fitness center. *Info: Tel. 866/237-3491. www.longbay.com.*

Peter Island $$$$

This is true luxury: a resort that occupies a private island. With 52 guest rooms and three villas, Peter Island is truly a place where

relaxation can flourish like the bougainvillea, hibiscus, and sea grapes that dot its hills. This 1,800-acre island is paradise for those seeking relaxation. It starts with your arrival by private launch from Tortola, and continues as you check in and see your guest room: a combination of Scandinavian and Caribbean styles. Complimentary activities include snorkeling, tennis, hobie cats, Laser sailboats, tennis, Sunfish, kayaks, windsurfing, mountain biking, and more. If all that activity puts you in the mood to really relax, The Spa at Peter Island, which opened in 2004, has 10 treatment rooms and two outdoor treatment bohios that overlook the sea. Look for signature treatments that include Thermal Sand Bundle Massage, West Indian Honey & Sesame Seed Glow, Frangipani & Coconut Moisturizer and Thalasso Mud Bowls Alfresco. *Info: Tel. 800/346-4451, 284/495-2000 , www.peterisland.com.*

Rosewood Little Dix Bay $$$$
We have fond memories of our stay at Rosewood Little Dix on Virgin Gorda: lazing beneath a palm palapa, snorkeling just offshore, enjoying our rondoval guest room with a wonderful view in every direction, dining outdoors to the music of whistling tree frogs.

Apparently plenty of other travelers also have good memories of Little Dix; it boasts a wonderful repeat business. Many customers have been coming since the days Laurance Rockefeller first developed this property in 1964. Today the hotel still has the same attention to service as it did in its Rockresort days; you'll find that the ratio of employees to guests is one to one. Although much has stayed the same, look for additions and improvements to the property as well including Sense, a luxurious spa perched on a cliff overlooking the Sir Francis Drake

SLEEPS & EATS

Channel. Signature treatments include the Virgin Gorda Goat Milk & Honey Wrap and the Salt Island Scrub. The spa also includes a two-tier infinity pool and a Cliff Spa Suite available for couples. *Info: Tel. 888/ROSEWOOD or 284/495-5555, www.littledixbay.com.*

The Sugar Mill Hotel $$$-$$$$

If you're a cooking aficionado, you may already be familiar with the Sugar Mill's owners, Jinx and Jeff Morgan. These *Bon Appetit* columnists and cookbook authors have brought their expertise to the Caribbean in the Sugar Mill Restaurant (see Best Eats, below.) But part of the recipe for happiness for this former California couple included not just a restaurant but a complete resort. Since 1982, the Morgans have operated this inn and made it a prime destination for travelers looking for peace and privacy. Today The Sugar Mill is one of the finest small inns in the Caribbean, offering visitors a chance to enjoy a spectacular setting while at the same time feeling part of island life.

It's those grounds that draw visitors to this Tortola site. This hotel is located on the ruins of the Appleby Plantation, which dates back to this island's days of sugar and slaves. Little remains of the early buildings except the ruins of a 360-year-old sugar mill, today part of the hotel's elegant restaurant. Another reminder of the location's sugar history is the swimming pool. This circular tank is built on the site of a treadmill where oxen once powered the machinery to crush the sugar cane that eventually became rum. *Info: 800/462-8834 (US), 800/209-6874 (Canada), 284/495-4355, www.sugarmillhotel.com.*

Toad Hall $$$$

This elegant villa offers its guests privacy and one-of-a-kind rooms where you'll truly feel like you're living outdoors.

Scattered among the six and a half acres are three guest suites, bath cottages with stone showers tucked into screened gardens (and one with a whirlpool bath), dining room, kitchen, and living room. The real treat is the location: perched just above The Baths this inn has the only private access to the park beach. The atmosphere of The Baths is felt here at the inn as well; granite boulders tumble from the sides of the swimming pool, mimicking the natural pools just down the hill. *Info: Tel. 284/495-5397, www.toadhallvg.com.*

Eclipse Restaurant $$$$
This dinner-only restaurant is tucked right on the waterfront, the perfect end to a day of sailing or other watersports. Look for an elegant menu featuring entrees such as Filetto Cambozola, a chargrilled bacon-wrapped filet mignon topped with cambozola and served with a red wine jus or Shrimp Rumaki, jumbo prawns wrapped around fresh pineapple, rolled in prosciutto and served with a carrot chipotle syrup. *Info: Penn's Landing Marina, East End, Tortola, Tel. 284/495-1646, www.eclipse-restaurant.com.*

BVI CUISINE

Before dinner, many vacationers stop off at their resort or a local bar for a sample of a true BVI product: **Pusser's Rum**. The most popular drink is the Painkiller, made from Pusser's Rum, orange and pineapple juice, and coconut crème.

There's really no need to worry about a painkiller, though, because dinner in the BVI is a painless affair. Restaurants here are typically very casual, usually outdoors, and feature excellent cuisine. Fresh fish as well as lobster and conch are specialties in most restaurants. Curried dishes are favorites as well.

Pusser's Landing Bar & Restaurant $$-$$$
A favorite stop with boaters thanks to its waterfront location, the outdoor bar here serves up plenty of the local specialty: Pusser's

SLEEPS & EATS

Rum. Upstairs, the restaurant serves a varied menu including local catch, Caribbean lobster, pineapple-ginger grilled chicken, blackened NY Strip steak, curried shrimp, and more. Save room for the big array of desserts including Blue Mountain Mud Pie and Banana Rum Crisp. *Info: Soper's Hole, Tortola, Tel. 284/495-4603, www.pussers.com.*

Sugar Mill Restaurant $$$-$$$$

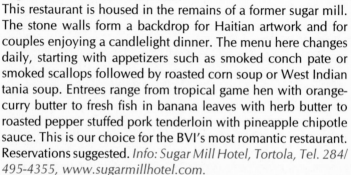

This restaurant is housed in the remains of a former sugar mill. The stone walls form a backdrop for Haitian artwork and for couples enjoying a candlelight dinner. The menu here changes daily, starting with appetizers such as smoked conch pate or smoked scallops followed by roasted corn soup or West Indian tania soup. Entrees range from tropical game hen with orange-curry butter to fresh fish in banana leaves with herb butter to roasted pepper stuffed pork tenderloin with pineapple chipotle sauce. This is our choice for the BVI's most romantic restaurant. Reservations suggested. *Info: Sugar Mill Hotel, Tortola, Tel. 284/495-4355, www.sugarmillhotel.com.*

PRACTICAL MATTERS

Currency. The US dollar is legal tender here.

Driving. Driving is on the LEFT side of the road.

Electricity. 110 volts, 60 cycles throughout the islands.

Getting There. Connecting service to Tortola's Terrence B. Lettsome International Airport (formerly Beef Island International Airport) is available from several Caribbean airports but there is no direct service from the US mainland or Canada. Many vacationers prefer to fly directly into St. Thomas and ferry to Tortola, or into Puerto Rico and then take a small plane.

Information. British Virgin Islands Tourist Board, *Tel. 800/835-8530 or 284/494-3134*

Website. *www.bvitourism.com*

PRACTICAL MATTERS

7. CAYMAN ISLANDS

For the American traveler, perhaps no other Caribbean islands offer the comforts and "this is almost like back home" feeling of the **Cayman Islands**, especially the most popular destination: Grand Cayman. This island, together with its smaller cousins,

Cayman Brac and **Little Cayman**, enjoys the highest per capita income in the Caribbean, is friendly, safe, and tailor-made for couples looking for a slice of home on their vacation. Here you'll find all the comforts of the US, as well as an American standard of service in many restaurants, bars, and hotels from many stateside ex-pats who make their home in these lovely isles. For some visitors, this Americanized atmosphere is as welcome as eating a Big Mac in Paris; for others it is a comforting way to experience the islands.

INTRO

All that comfort referred to on the previous page comes at a price, however. The Cayman dollar is stronger than its US equivalent. Prices in hotels, restaurants, shops, and attractions reflect that unfavorable exchange rate and high standard of living.

These lofty price tags don't deter the vacationers and businesspeople who fly into these islands every year. The vacationers are drawn by protected waters as clear as white rum and teeming with marine life, offering one of the best snorkeling and scuba vacations in the region. The business world is attracted to these small islands for an entirely different reason: tax free status. (Remember *The Firm*? Portions of that movie, based on the John Grisham book, were filmed right here.)

The three islands, although similar in terrain, flora, and fauna, are vastly different in atmosphere. None of the Cayman Islands offer a rollicking experience of around-the-clock excitement, casino action, or frenetic shopping; travelers head to other islands for those experiences. But for those looking for luxurious resorts, seaside golf, a little nightlife, and a somewhat party atmosphere, **Grand Cayman** is the choice. Here a large list of watersports operators offers every type of underwater and on the water adventure you could want. Restaurants and bars line busy Seven Mile Beach, and vacationers from around the globe fill hotels, condominiums, time shares, motels, and accommodations for most budgets. The largest of the three islands, Grand Cayman offers several types of experiences, though, from fun-loving **Seven Mile Beach** to quiet, little changed East End to historic **George Town**.

On the other hand, if you're looking for seclusion, a real getaway, head to the Sister Islands: **Little Cayman** and **Cayman Brac**. These islands are true hideaways, places for those who want to get away from the crowd. You'll find dive operators, fishing guides, and charter boats on these tiny isles as well and adventure around every bend.

Whichever your choice, you're never limited to just one destination in the Cayman Islands. These isles are much smaller than their easterly neighbors such as Cuba and Jamaica. You do not need to choose only one area or even one island for your vacation.

Grand Cayman visitors find that they can easily maneuver the entire landmass in one day. The island of Grand Cayman is shaped somewhat like a wrench, lying on its side with the jaws facing upwards or north. The handle of the wrench is the East End. A main road circles the entire East End, running east from George Town, tracing the shoreline as it snakes through small communities such as **Bodden Town** and **Spotts**. This road turns north at the end of the island and begins to trace the northern edge of the island, but you can take a shortcut halfway down the island on the **Frank Sound Road**, the route to the **Queen Elizabeth II Botanic Gardens**.

Picturing the wrench, the North Sound lies between the wrench's open jaws. Where this body of water meets the sea is the home of **Stingray City**, a must-do for any Cayman visitor, diver or not. Returning to the wrench, picture the top jaw of the tool. As it turns away from the handle, this is the location of George Town, the capital of the Cayman Islands. Home of the international airport, most visitors start their stay in this clean, orderly community.

From George Town, **Seven Mile Beach** sprawls to the north, tucked between the sea and the North Sound. This narrow strip of land may be small but its not short in accommodations and restaurants; this is the heart of vacationland. Finally, Seven Mile Beach ends in **West Bay**, the clump of land on the westernmost side of the North Sound.

And while Grand Cayman offers plenty of activity for even the most action-packed vacation, don't feel like you're bound by this 76-square-mile island. It's a short hop from George Town to either of the Sister Islands for an overnight stay or just a day trip. Also inter-island flights connect Little Cayman and Cayman Brac to each other, so any vacationer can, on any given day, do a little island hopping for a totally different experience.

Transportation in the Cayman Islands is easy. Take your pick from taxis and group tours as well as rental cars, vans, jeeps, and sedans. On Grand Cayman, 4x4 vehicles are commonplace and many travelers enjoy driving around the island in the open-air vehicles. Air-conditioned sedans are also commonplace and often a better choice for families and those who want to secure their valuables while at the beach or in town. Most agencies feature American and Japanese models. Some offer unlimited mileage, free pickup and dropoff and free airport transfers.

SIGHTS

BEST SIGHTS IN CAYMAN ISLANDS

George Town, the capital city, is home to the **Cayman Islands National Museum**, *Harbour Drive, Tel. 345/949-8368, www.museum.ky*. The Cayman Islands National Museum is, in our opinion, one of the finest museums in the Caribbean. A visit here is a great way to learn more about Cayman history and culture.

Over the years, this seaside building, just across from the cruise ship terminals, has served as a courthouse, jail, and meeting hall, and today it houses over 2,000 artifacts that recall the history of these islands. Created in 1979 by a museum law and opened in 1990, the museum collects items of historic, scientific, and artistic relevance.

Some of the most fascinating displays recall the early economy of the Caymanians. An oral history program reveals the history of early turtlers who made a living capturing the now protected reptiles. Exhibits show the tools of the early residents such as the muntle, a club used to kill fish, the calabash, a versatile gourd that once dried had many uses, sisal switches used to beat mosquitoes away, and wompers, sandals worn on the East End, originally made from leather and later from old tires.

After your museum tour, you'll exit through the museum shop, a good source of Cayman-made items. The shop, housed in the old jail with part of the old coral stone wall still exposed, has a good selection of books and maps of the Cayman Islands. (If you don't have time for a museum tour, you can enter through the store for a little shopping.) History buffs will also enjoy a visit to **Pedro St. James**, *Tel. 9 4 7 - 3 3 2 9 , www.pedrostjames.ky*, located east of the capital city. The National Historic Site, called the Birthplace of Democracy in the Cayman Islands, includes a 1780 greathouse, expansive lawn area, and multi-media theater. Called **Pedro Castle**, the historic structure is located in the community of Savannah, east of George Town.

The oldest known stone structure in the Cayman Islands, Pedro Castle was first built in the late 18th century as a great house for William Eden, an early settler. In 1831, the house was the site of an historic meeting when residents decided that the five districts should have representation in the government. Four years later, a proclamation declaring the emancipation of all slaves was read at Pedro Castle and at several other sites in the islands.

Restorating the castle was a major undertaking, costing US $6.25 million; the project was completed in December 1998. The site is at the center of a 7.65 acre landscaped park atop the 30-foot Great Pedro Bluff. For the past several years, historic research into the site has been conducted.

Continuing east, the **Queen Elizabeth Botanic Park**, *Tel. 947-9462, www.botanic-park.ky*, is filled with native trees, wild orchids, as well as birds, reptiles, and butterflies. Here you can enjoy a self-guided tour and a quiet look at the flora and fauna that make the Cayman Islands special.

From the North Side most tours travel to the East End,

SIGHTS

home of the **Blow Holes**. Park and walk down to the rugged coral rocks that have been carved by the rough waves into caverns. As waves hit the rocks, water spews into the air, creating one of the best photo sites on the island.

Continuing past George Town lies **Boatswain's Beach and the Cayman Turtle Farm**, West Bay, *Tel. 949-3894; www.turtle.ky*, one of the Caribbean's most popular attractions. The Cayman Turtle Farm is now part of Boatswain's Beach, an extensive facility spanning 23 acres that includes swimming, shopping, and other activities. Along with the turtles,

you'll find a caiman exhibit; spectacled caiman (not a native species) are on display, representative of the now extinct caiman for which the islands are named.

There's no visiting Grand Cayman without seeing what lies beneath the water's surface. But you don't even have to get wet to enjoy the underwater sights of the Caribbean. The **Atlantis submarine**, George Town, *Tel. 800/887-8571*, offers hourly dives six days a week. For 50 minutes, you'll feel like an underwater explorer as you dive to a depth of 100 feet below the surface. It's a unique opportunity to view colorful coral formations and sponge gardens, and identify hundreds of varieties of tropical fish. The submarine has individual porthole windows for each passenger, plus cards to help you identify fish species. A pilot and co-pilot point out attractions during the journey.

Another option is the **Seaworld Observatory**, located next to Atlantis Submarine on South Church Street. Like the Nautilus, it is a good option for those who might feel a little claustrophobic about a submarine adventure (it does not go below the water's surface). Visitors descend into a glass observatory and view marine life as well as two shipwrecks. The Explorer travels to the Cali, a schooner that hit the reef in 1944, and the Balboa, a freighter from Cuba destroyed by a hurricane. Today the wrecks are encased in corals and filled with fish life. Seaworld Explorer tours last one hour.

A sunset cruise may be pure heaven, but one of Grand Cayman's top tourist spots is pure **Hell**. This odd attraction is actually a community named **Hell**, a moniker derived from the devilishly pointed rocks near town, a bed of limestone and dolomite that through millions of years eroded into a crusty, pocked formation locally called ironshore.

Today, Hell trades upon its unusual name as a way to draw tourists to the far end of west Bay. The Devil's Hangout Gift Shop (open daily) is manned by Ivan Farrington, who dresses as the devil himself to greet tourists who come to buy the obligatory post-

card and have it postmarked from Hell.

There's no doubt that one of the top draws of Grand Cayman is the unparalleled **scuba diving** in its clear waters. With visibility often exceeding 100 feet, this is a diver's paradise with over 130 sites to select from near Grand Cayman. Wall and reef dives, many less than half a mile from shore are available as well from many operators including Don Foster's Dive Cayman, *Tel. 949-5679*, Red Sail Sports, *Tel. 877/RED-SAIL* and many more.

The top underwater attraction on Grand Cayman is **Stingray City**, the place to act out your Jacques Cousteau fantasies. It's an area where numerous operators (including many of the scuba operators named above) introduce vacationers to one of the most unique experiences in the Caribbean.

Following a short boat ride, visitors don snorkel gear and swim with the stingrays just offshore on a shallow sandbar. Accustomed to being fed, the stingrays (which range in size from about one to six feet across) are docile and friendly, brushing against swimmers and even allowing themselves to be held and petted. About 30 stingrays frequent this area. Even non-swimmers can enjoy the experience.

BEST FESTIVAL

At the end of October, it's shiver-me-timbers time during **Pirates Week**. The islands celebrate their buccaneering history with treasure hunts, parades, and plenty of excuses to dress as pirates and wenches.

BEST SHOPPING

Almost all the shopping in the Cayman Islands is found on **Grand Cayman** and most of that is in **George Town**. Duty-free shopping is especially popular in George Town where you can choose from china, perfumes, leather goods, watches, crystal, and more.

If you're looking for something uniquely Caymanian, check out the **Caymanite jewelry**. Made from a stone found only on the eastern end of Grand Cayman and on Cayman Brac, Caymanite somewhat resembles tiger's eye.

BEST SPORTS & RECREATION

One of the most fascinating features of **Boatswain's Beach** is its **snorkeling facility**, a million-gallon lagoon that's home to 14,000 fish as well as four dry islands. The lagoon features an artificial reef populated by species indigenous to the Cayman Islands.

Also here you'll find **Breaker's Beach**, a 300,000-gallon swimming pool with rockwork constructed to resemble the cliffs of Cayman Brac. The best feature of the pool is its window, an underwater viewing panel that looks right into the **Predator Tank**, letting swimmers swim just four inches from the tank's sharks. Along with sandbar and nurse sharks, the predator tank is also home to tarpon and jacks.

When it's time to get out of the water, visitors can explore the park's hiking trail which features local karst formations and native plants. And for a little more landlubber activity, you'll find shopping kiosks and a large gift shop on the property.

BEST SLEEPS & EATS

Grand Cayman Marriott Beach Resort $$$
Located two miles from George Town and about four miles from
the airport, this convenient property (formerly the Radisson) sits

on a beautiful stretch
of Seven Mile Beach.
In 2006, this property
underwent a $15 mil-
lion renovation and
redesign; the public
areas and guest rooms
are now done in so-
phisticated
Caymanian colors. All
guest rooms are now
smoke-free. Rooms and public areas feature high-speed wireless
internet connectivity. Oceanfront rooms have private balconies
with good beach views and are worth a somewhat long walk to
the elevators in this 309-room hotel. The hotel's expanded La
Mer Spa now includes four large treatment rooms and a couple's
suite with Jacuzzi.

The hotel's four restaurants and bars were renovated as well.
Options now include Solana on Seven Mile Beach for breakfast,
lunch, and dinner, Red Parrot (which offers a breakfast buffet as
well as evening steak and seafood option), a beach bar, and a
lounge.

The beach has been rejuvenated with the addition of $250,000
in reef balls which protect the beach sand as well as draw marine
life, enhancing the snorkeling opportunities. Facilities include a
freshwater pool and hot tub, dive shop, snorkeling, jet-skiing,
kayaking, waterskiing, and shopping arcade. *Info: Tel. 800/223-
6388 or 345/949-0088, www.marriott.com.*

The Ritz-Carlton, Grand Cayman $$$-$$$$
One of the island's most elegant resorts, the Ritz-Carlton offers
365 elegant rooms and suites on Seven Mile Beach. The hotel

offers many room types; the lowest priced are the Waterway rooms located on the North Sound side of the property; these rooms include a terrace and either two queen beds or a king bed with  loveseat sofa. Oceanfront rooms are the second category with views of the sea as well as the terrace and same bed configuration. Slightly more expensive are the Waterway Club Rooms with the same view as the Waterway rooms but with Club Level amenities including access to the Ritz-Carlton Club lounge which offers five food presentations per day. The property also offers suites and two- and three-bedroom accommodations in The Reserve featuring private oceanfront units.

The resort includes Blue Tip, a Greg Norman-designed 3,515-yard, par 36 golf course. The facility also includes a pro shop, private and group instruction, and rental equipment. The resort is also home to a Nick Bollettieri tennis center (Nick Bollettieri has instructed Andre Agassi, Monica Seles and Maria Sharapova). For a little less activity, there's also a 6,000-square-foot shopping emporium with duty free shopping.

The hotel is also home to Silver Rain, a La Prairie Spa created specifically for the resort. The $10 million spa has 17 treatment rooms and adjoins a full-service salon and fitness center.

In terms of dining, take your choice among two restaurants created by Eric Ripert of New York's Le Bernardin: Blue by Eric Ripert (see Best Eats, below) for fine seafood dining and the more casual Periwinkle by Eric Ripert for alfresco dining. Other dining options include an oceanfront café called 7 (which in the evening becomes 7 Prime Cuts & Sunsets). The Silver Palm offers light fare

SLEEPS & EATS

(including caviar, of course) along with champagne and wine while Bar Jack keeps guests hydrated at poolside. Guests also have access to 24-hour room service. *Info: Tel. 800/542-8680 or 345/943-9000, www.ritzcarlton.com.*

Westin Casuarina Resort & Spa, Grand Cayman $$$
This upscale beach resort is built on a strip of Seven Mile Beach bordered by willowy casuarina trees. The hotel has 343 guest rooms, most with breathtaking views of the sea from step-out balconies. The hotel has the feel of a conference property, with a slightly dress-up atmosphere in the main lobby. Facilities include beachfront, casual and fine dining restaurants, pools, whirlpools, tennis, fitness facilities, beauty salons, masseuse and masseur. *Info: Tel. 800/937-8461 or 345/945-3800, www.starwoodhotels.com.*

Blue by Eric Ripert $$$
Eric Ripert of New York's Le Bernardin has created Blue by Eric Ripert for fine seafood dining. Menus feature locally-caught seafood with a three-course prix fixe menu and six course tasting menu; you'll also find a wine cellar here featuring over 650 selections. Open for dinner only, Tuesday through Saturday. *Info: Ritz-Carlton, Grand Cayman, Tel. 345/943-9000.*

Lighthouse at Breakers $$
On the south shore about 25 minutes from George Town, this picturesque restaurant offers good seafood and Italian cuisine and an even better view. We dined on the open air back deck, a romantic spot for dinner or lunch. *Info: 20 minutes east of George Town, Tel. 345/947-2047, www.lighthouse.ky.*

CAYMAN DINING
Grand Cayman is filled with restaurants of every description, from fast food joints to fine dining. Check your bill before paying as some restaurants automatically add a 15 percent gratuity to the total.

Lobster Pot Restaurant and Wine Bar $$-$$$
This restaurant is known for its excellent view, an attentive staff, a good wine list, and a romantic atmosphere. We enjoyed a romantic dinner of, what else, Caribbean lobster

tail at this casually elegant restaurant overlooking the sea. Other popular dishes include cracked conch, island seafood curry with shrimp, fish, scallops, and lobster, Cayman turtle steak, and steak. *Info: 245 North Church Street, George Town, Tel. 345/ 949-2736, www.lobsterpot.ky.*

Periwinkle by Eric Ripert $$$
This alfresco restaurant, a casual option for visitors who might also enjoy Blue by Eric Ripert, also at this hotel, celebrates the Mediterranean roots of the chef. Reflecting the Andorran and Provencal heritage of Ripert, the menu offers seafood that has been out of the sea less than 24 hours, accompanied by the finest sea salt, seasonings, and olive oil. Dishes include yellowfin tuna with a mango Mostarda, mussels, chorizo steamed in white wine and herbs, and coconut marinated shrimp ceviche with mango, fresh chilies and herbs. Open for lunch and dinner. *Info: The Ritz-Carlton, Grand Cayman, Tel. 345/943-9000.*

PRACTICAL MATTERS

Currency. The official currency is the Cayman Dollar, exchanged at a rate of US $1 equals CI 80 cents.

Driving. Driving is British style, on the LEFT.

Getting There. You'll arrive in Grand Cayman at Owen Roberts International Airport. The major carrier into this port of entry is Cayman Airways, *Tel. 800/4CAYMAN*, the national carrier. Service is also available from major US and Canadian airlines. Direct flights to Cayman Brac are available.

Information. Cayman Islands Department of Tourism, *Tel. 877/ 4CAYMAN*

Website. *www.caymanislands.ky*

8. CURAÇAO

Just the name **Curaçao**—derived from the Portuguese word for the heart— speaks of romance. Add to that a historic capital city with tiny twinkling lights and picturesque European-style structures, fine cuisine from around the globe, and both tranquil beaches and rugged coastline, and you have all the ingredients for a romantic getaway.

Curaçao is part of the **Netherlands Antilles**, along with the islands of Sint Maarten, Bonaire, Saba, and St. Eustatius. The Netherlands Antilles, the island of Aruba, and Holland comprise the Kingdom of the Netherlands. Ruled by a governor appointed by the Queen, each island has autonomy on domestic affairs. Curaçao is the capital of the Netherlands Antilles, and here you'll find most of the governmental, financial, and industrial positions.

INTRO

Tucked into the far southern reaches of the Caribbean, less than 40 miles from the coast of South America, Curaçao is very much an international destination. **Dutch** is the official language, and you'll

hear many Dutch-speaking vacationers. Many South Americans also enjoy the island where most residents speak Spanish. We found that most Curaçao residents speak an amazing total of five languages: Dutch, Spanish, English, Papiamento, and either French or German.

Papiamento is the local language spoken on the streets, a veritable cocktail of tongues. Spanish, Portuguese, French, Dutch, Indian, English, and some African dialects combine to form the *lingua franca* of the Netherlands Antilles. Even between the islands the language varies slightly, each with its own slang and accent.

That ease with multiple languages also seems to translate into a comfort with many nationalities as well. Over 70 nationalities are represented on the island and, with such a true melting pot on this 184-square-mile piece of land, there's a true welcoming spirit for tourists, wherever their homeland. When Curaçoans says "Bon Bini," they mean welcome in any language.

On one side of the island lies the capital of **Willemstad**, a truly international city with streets lined with Dutch-style architecture as colorful as a candy store. The city is divided into two sides: Punda, the original settlement, and Otrobanda, literally the "other side." Both sport picturesque harborfront buildings, and are connected by the largest bridge in the Caribbean, a free ferry, and the Queen Emma Pontoon Bridge for pedestrians, locally known as the "Swinging Old Lady" because of the way it moves out of the way for harbor traffic.

Beyond Willemstad, Curaçao becomes a three-tiered countryside dotted with tall cacti trimmed with coastlines of the windswept and tranquil varieties. The Atlantic shoreline of the island is rugged and wild, with pounding surf, shady sea caves, and evidence of past volcanic action. Swimming is prohibited in the dangerous waters, but swimmers will find plenty of calm waters along the placid Caribbean side of the island.

Getting around is best accomplished by taxi if you'll be staying in Willemstad; if you make a home base elsewhere on the island, a rental car is useful. Taxi service is easily available.

BEST SIGHTS IN CURACAO

SIGHTS

Start with a visit to **Willemstad**, a historic city that bustles with activity but also takes a slower pace in its shopping district. Here you can take a guided tour aboard an open-air trolley or a self-guided walk for a look at Fort Amsterdam. And you can't miss the historic harborside shops, as colorful as Easter eggs.

Stroll through the streets and alleyways, then walk across the Wilhelmina Bridge to the **Floating Market**, one of Willemstad's most colorful sites. Here Venezuelans sell fresh fish and vegetables (a real commodity on an island without much agriculture). Stroll along the waterway booths and buy exotic tropical fruits or watch fishermen cleaning their catch for a buyer. Behind the stalls, col-orful schooners make an excellent photo.

While you're in the city, make time for a visit to **Seaquarium**, *Bapor Kibra, Tel. 011/5999-461-6666,* one of the Caribbean's finest marine exhibits and a definite winner. Along with tanks of local fish, coral, and sponges, the aquarium also has several outdoor tanks with larger species—including sharks, sea turtles, and stingrays. Divers and would-be divers can take a dip here and feed the sharks through holes in an underwater Plexiglass wall. Complete

instruction and equipment are provided. For those who want a drier look at these toothy denizens, just walk down into the Seaquarium Explorer, a semi-submarine parked by the shark tank. Half-day and full-day encounters allow you to make contact with such sea-dwellers as dolphins, invertebrates and even the dangers of the deep, sharks.

Curaçao may be a dry, desert island, but you'll find plenty of other natural attractions. One is **Boca Tabla**, a sea cave carved by pounding Atlantic waves. Located on the road to Westpoint, the cave is a short walk off the road (wear sturdy shoes!). Kneeling in the darkness of the sea cave, you'll watch the surge of crystal blue waves as they come within feet of you, roaring into the cave and back out to sea.

Above the cave, walk on the volcanic rock (stay on the pebble path) to the seaside cliffs for excellent photos.

If you'd like to venture into a cavern, take a tour of **Hato Caves**, open daily except Monday. Guided tours take you through the stalactite and stalagmite filled rooms, several of which include pools or waterfalls.

Nature lovers should save time for a visit to **Christoffel National Park**, on the western end of the island. This wildlife preserve includes the island's highest point and 20 miles of trails that wind through local flora and fauna. Don't be surprised to see some native wildlife in the park; it is home to iguanas, donkeys, small deer, rabbits, and many bird species.

BEST SHOPPING

Curaçao's shopping opportunities keep many travelers busy, especially in downtown **Willemstad**. The prime shopping district is in **Punda**, just across the floating bridge. Cross the bridge and continue up **Breede Straat**, where you'll find most of the shops and boutiques aimed at vacationers, along with some charming sidewalk cafes.

The most obvious shop in Punda is the **J.L. Penha and Sons** department store, housed

in a beautiful lemon-tinted colonial building constructed in 1708. You'll find just about everything in this department store, from perfumes to fine jewelry to collectibles.

Down **Breede Straat**, look for Caribbean collectibles, spices, and crafts. The Gomezplein plaza, just a couple of blocks up from the bridge, offers picturesque boutiques and a relaxed shopping atmosphere.

For lower priced purchases, take a turn off Breede Straat and enjoy a stroll down **Heeren Straat** or **Keuken Straat**. These streets are filled with electronics, inexpensive clothing, and housewares. It's a fun atmosphere where you'll have a chance to mix with residents.

These streets end at the water, where you'll find an entirely different shopping opportunity: the **Floating Market**. Schooners from Venezuela bring exotic fruits, vegetables, spices, and plants to this open-air market that's very popular with older residents. To reach the floating market, walk across the bridge at Columbus Straat. We highly recommend the market to enjoy a slice of island life and, for the photographers out there, to capture one of Curaçao's most colorful sights.

BEST SPORTS & RECREATION

After the Seaquarium have a dip at the **Seaquarium Beach**, a full-service beach with watersports, restaurant, bar, and plenty of action. There's a

small admission charge. This is the beach where Curaçaoans and visitors come to see and be seen. Waters as calm as a lake make swimming inside the breakwaters delightful.

Curaçao has over three dozen additional beaches from which to choose, all on the Caribbean side of the island. Some of the most popular are **Knip Bay** and **Barbara Beach**.

BEST FESTIVALS

Curaçao's **Carnival** is a top draw and brings in travelers from near and far. Ending with Ash Wednesday, the Carnival's final parade is the culmination of almost two months of partying. For travelers, the **Kaya 9** is a special day of festival aimed at visitors with parades, plenty of music, the appearance of Carnival Queen and Tumba King and Queen, and more. Check with the tourist board for the scheduling of Kaya 9, usually held a few weeks before the culmination of Carnival.

BEST SLEEPS & EATS

Breezes Curaçao Resort, Spa & Casino $$
The top all-inclusive resort in Curaçao, this resort is located two miles from Willemstad. The expansive resort offers a 12,000-square-foot kids' club, water sports, tennis courts, beach volleyball, bicycles, fitness center, three pools, Jacuzzis, and a spa. With complimentary snorkeling and one included shore dive per day, guests can explore colorful Curaçao from above or below the water. *Info: Tel. 800/GO-SUPER, www.superclubs.com.*

Hilton Curaçao $$$
Located four miles from Willemstad, the 196-room hotel boasts two private white sand beaches. The hotel is home to the first LivingWell Health and Beach Club in the world and the first LivingWell Club of any kind in the Caribbean. The facility includes pools, tennis, a fitness area, and fitness classes as well as an extensive spa. *Info: Tel. 877/GO-HILTON or 011/5999-462-5000, www.hiltoncaribbean.com.*

SLEEPS & EATS

Hotel Kura Hulanda Spa & Casino $$$

Hotel Kurá Hulanda, a member of Leading Small Hotels of the World, is a 100-room luxury urban resort located within an eight-

block village/complex, which is being lovingly restored by Jacob Gelt Dekker. Within this village are several outstanding properties all developed by Dr. Dekker, including the Museum Kurá Hulanda. The hotel village, spread over an eight-block area, includes two pools, numerous restaurants and bars, shops, a spa, casino, and more. *Info: Tel. 877/264-3106 or 011/5999-434-7700, www.kurahulanda.com.*

Lodge Kura Hulanda and Beach Club $$-$$$

Featuring a beautiful soft white sand beach and a spectacular swimming pool, this quiet resort is a sister property to Hotel Kura Hulanda Spa & Casino. The lodge's 74 villas and suites are located on the western end of the island approximately 20 minutes from the airport. Complimentary shuttle service is available to Hotel Kura Hulanda Spa & Casino. *Info: Tel. 877/ 264-3106 or 011/5999-434-7700, www.kurahulanda.com.*

Marriott Curacao Beach Resort & Emerald Casino $$$

This 247-room resort (formerly the Sonesta) is a AAA four-diamond property, an elegant resort with a Dutch Caribbean style. Cool lemon walls contrast with chile pepper-colored roofs, all framed by stately palms. The property is a veritable oasis on this dry island. We especially liked the low-rise, open-air quality of this resort, starting with the lobby, where you'll arrive to a view over a cascading fountain across the palm-shaded pool and out to the sea. Every room includes either a balcony or patio (ask for a ground floor room for direct beach access) and at least a partial view of the ocean. *Info: Tel 011/5999-736-8800 or 800/223-6388, www.curacaomarriott.com.*

Renaissance Curaçao Resort & Casino $$-$$$
The 237-room Renaissance Curaçao Resort & Casino opened in February 2009 as the island's first new branded hotel in 15 years. The resort, which is connected to Rif Fort, a 19th century landmark and UNESCO World Heritage site. The resort features a 15,000-square-foot casino and spa, and will include a mall with six theaters and 50 shops. The Aqua Spa is an 8,300-square-foot health and wellness center spanning three floors of the resort; it features a roof top relaxation area and an infinity pool hot tub overlooking the ocean and passing cruise ships.

A unique feature of this resort is its signature white sand "Eternity Beach." The creation of modern maritime engineering and the only one in the world, this beach sits above sea level and is located adjacent to the resort's freshwater infinity pool. *Info: Tel. 888/778-4722, www.renaissancecuracao.com.*

Bistro le Clochard $$$
Located in the Rif Fort, this elegant restaurant features Swiss and French cuisines and is often lauded as the island's best dining option. Look for entrees including veal goulash served with homemade spinach noodles, roasted rack of lamb with rosemary oil, ratatouille and blue cheese and potato gratin, a variety of steaks, broiled salmon steak served with a creamy lobster sauce, and both cheese and beef fondues. *Info: Rif Fort, Willemstad, Tel. 011/5999-462-5666, www.bistroleclochard.com.*

CURACAO DINING
With its numerous nationalities, Curaçao enjoys many cuisines. **Indonesian rijstaffel** or rice table is especially popular. Local specialties include *stoba di cabrito* (goat stew), fried plantains, seafood, and conch or *karko*. Amstel beer, Dutch gin, and local rums such as San Pablo are choice drinks. For an after-dinner liqueur, try Senior Curaçao's Blue Curaçao (it comes in several other colors as well.) Made from a bitter orange grown on the island, select from flavors including orange, chocolate, rum raisin, and coffee.

SLEEPS & EATS

Fort Nassau $$-$$$
The most romantic night view in Willemstad is from this historic fort. Dine indoors or out on continental dishes at your table lit by

candlelight. Enjoy dishes as varied as *saltimbocca* (veal cutlets with sage and proscuitto) or fried sunfish breaded with pecan nuts, served with a choice of excellent soups such as mustard or rich coconut. *Info: Otrabanda, Willemstad, Tel. 011/5998-461-3450.*

Portofino Restaurant $$-$$$
This elegant restaurant features a new menu that combines flavors from European, Asian, and Caribbean cuisine. Look for options including filet mignon with Gouda cheese, Asian duck spring rolls, and orange-flavored chicken. *Info: Curaçao Marriott Beach Resort & Emerald Casino, Tel. 011/5999-736-8800.*

 ## PRACTICAL MATTERS

Currency. The official currency is the Antillean guilder, exchanged at a rate of US $1 = ANG 1.77.

Driving. Driving is on the right side of the road.

Electricity. Curaçao operates at 110-130 volts alternating current, 50 cycles, a little different from the US.

Getting There. Curaçao International Airport lies just minutes from Willemstad and the nearby resort hotels.

Information. Curaçao Tourist Board, *Tel. 800/CURACAO*

Website. *www.curacao.com*

PRACTICAL MATTERS

9. DOMINICAN REPUBLIC

For travelers on a budget, the **Dominican Republic** or Dominicana (not to be confused with Dominica, a somewhat remote island known for its eco-tourism) is an excellent choice. It is one of the least expensive Caribbean destinations, some sources estimating it to be as much as 50 to 70 percent cheaper than its neighbors, although increasingly work is beginning on luxury resorts with new developments by Aman, Fairmont, Four Seasons, Ritz Carlton, and Westin brand hotels on the island's east coast. The new constructions are part of expansive developments at Roco Ki and Cap Cana, as well as Costa Blanca near Juan Dolio.

Although values abound on this festive island, you needn't worry that you'll be shortchanged in terms of beauty or fun. The Dominican Republic has ancient history, mountain-covered vistas, and a party atmosphere that's as fun as any found throughout the Caribbean.

INTRO

Many resorts are found on the Dominican Republic's north side, a region dubbed the Amber Coast. The Dominican Republic boasts the fastest growing tourism business in the Caribbean, with over two million visitors a year. Over 60 percent of the vacationers are European.

For visitors, the two primary destinations in DR are Puerto Plata on the island's north shore and Punta Cana, on the eastern side of the island. Santo Domingo is located on the island's southern shore. Here history buffs will find a wealth of Spanish Renaissance architecture to explore. The city was the first permanent European settlement in the New World and has been honored for its cultural landmarks by a United Nations proclamation.

With 12,000 miles of roads, getting around the Dominican Republic can be achieved many different ways. You can rent a car from a major agency at the airports and in the larger cities. You'll need your driver's license and a major credit card. You'll also need good reflexes to deal with the frequent displays of driving *machismo* you will encounter. One fortunate thing: driving is (more or less) on the right side.

Taxis are a safer bet, but are fairly expensive and are unmetered; you'll need to negotiate a price before you embark. A variety of buses are also available from luxury lines to those with few creature comforts. The most basic transportation in the DR are the *guaguas,* unregulated taxi/buses which are usually crowded with locals. If you speak Spanish, riding the *guaguas* can be a good way to get the lowdown on what's happening.

BEST SIGHTS IN THE DOMINICAN REPUBLIC

SIGHTS

Jurassic Park buffs have come to the right place. Amber-encased specimens were borrowed from the collection of Puerto Plata's **Amber Museum,** *Tel. 809/586-2848, www.ambermuseum.com,* to make the movie and today you can have a look at amber-encased mosquitoes, termites, ants, fern, cockroaches, and even a tiny lizard. This Caribbean nation is one of only a few sites on the globe where amber is found.

Housed in a two story Victorian structure, the museum features amber mined in the Septentrional mountains along the north coast. The museum was founded by Didi and Aldo Costa. Their collection of amber is the most extensive in the world.

When removed from the geologic layers on the mountainside, amber looks like an unspectacular stone. Cutting and polishing, however, reveals its true nature — not a stone at all but a translucent fossilized sap. Amber ranges in color from pale yellow to dark brown, depending on the surrounding soil. A rare blue tinted amber is colored by volcanic gas. The most treasured pieces of amber are those that have "inclusions" — leaves, insects or even small reptiles trapped in these crystal coffins.

The Amber Museum has numerous displays of amber and provides guided tours in several languages, including English. After a tour of the museum, most visitors head to the shop downstairs (even larger than the museum). Here shoppers find one of the north

SIGHTS

coast's largest selections of amber jewelry.

Dating back to the 16th century, the **Fortaleza San Felipe** still stands guard over the city and the harbor. Built by the Spaniards to protect the city from pirates; in this century it was used as a prison. The doors within the fort are only four feet tall, slowing down would-be attackers (and keeping tourists alert). The fort includes a small museum with a collection of period weapons and cannon balls.

Another fort stands at the top of **Pico Isabel de Torres**, one of the highest points in the Dominican Republic. The dome-shaped fortress is topped with a statue of Christ similar to one that overlooks Rio de Janeiro.

In Santo Domingo, historic attractions fill the **Colonial Zone**. Tour sites such as the Catedral Santa Maria la Menor, the first cathedral in the Americas and, according to some historians, the final resting site of Christopher Columbus. Once mantilla-wearing ladies of the Spanish court paraded in their finery

along **Calle Las Damas**, the oldest street in the New World. The island also has a long history as a honeymoon haven — Columbus's son, Diego, first brought his new bride here half a millennium ago. Today that romantic Spanish heritage tempts lovers to stroll hand-in-hand along the narrow streets.

Near Casa de Campo, **Altos de Chavon** (*photo below*) is well worth a visit. This re-

creation of a 16th century art colony, complete with Spanish wrought ironwork and hushed courtyards, speaks of colonial style in a way no museum ever could.

BEST SHOPPING

The most unique purchase in the Dominican Republic is **amber**, available at gift shops along the north coast. Amber prices vary from US $3 for small earrings to US $200 for a mosquito encased in amber to several hundred dollars for large, chunky necklaces or amber set in gold. The color of the amber affects the price as well. Generally the pale blonde amber is the least expensive.

Amber resembles plastic, so avoid buying from street vendors and check your item before purchasing. Amber possesses a slight electromagnetic charge, so genuine amber, when rubbed on a piece of cloth, should attract particles. Better stores, such as the **Amber Museum Shop**, also have an ultraviolet light for testing. Genuine pieces will glow under the light. Also, amber will float in salt water while plastic will sink.

BEST SPORTS & RECREATION

Casa de Campo is known as one of the top **golf** areas in the country (*photo below*). New courses include Cap Cana's

Punta Espada, the DR's first signature Jack Nicklaus course, and Roco Ki's **Nick Faldo's Faldo Legacy Course**.

BEST FESTIVALS
Usually scheduled for late October/early November, the **Dominican Republic Jazz Festival** has grown to be the DR's largest and one of its best-loved special events. Top names in the jazz world are featured at the concerts in Santo Domingo and festival goers from around the world fly in for the three-day event.

BEST SLEEPS & EATS

Zoetry Agua Punta Cana $$$$
Located outside Punta Cana, this luxury resort is styled like a jungle getaway—but with lots of luxury. Thatched roof palapas

house air-conditioned rooms with LCD flat screen televisions with DVD players, in-room safe deposit boxes, minibars, a la carte pillows, Frette linens, Korres amenities and Wifi. You'll be pampered with 24-hour room service and twice daily maid service. The resort, composed of 53 suites in 18 villas, offers 24-hour butler service, two restaurants, two pools, and the option of private helicopter transfers to the airport. *Info: Tel. 888/4ZOETRY, www.zoetryresorts.com.*

Barcelo Bavaro Palace $$
This Punta Cana resort has reopened following a multi-million dollar addition of 488 new junior suites and the renovation of all existing guest rooms and public spaces. The all-inclusive resort

now features 1,046 deluxe guest rooms and junior suites; all junior suites offer a private balcony or terrace with whirlpool, 32" LCD televisions, high-speed wireless Internet access, and a large, spa-style bathroom. The resort features an 18-hole golf course, casino, spa, three theaters, 14 restaurants, and more. *Info: Tel. 800/BARCELO, www.barcelo.com.*

Casa de Campo $$$-$$$$

Located in La Romana, Casa de Campo is the Dominican

Republic's most lavish resort is also one of the most activity-oriented in the Carib-bean. You name it, you can do it at the plush resort sprawled over 7000 acres. Casa de Campo has added the Cygalle Healing Spa, offering eco-friendly holistic treatments and natural products made onsite in the spa pharmacy, and the Beach Club by Le Cirque, featuring a chef from New York's Le Cirque restaurant. Casa de Campo, with accommodations ranging from hotel rooms to villas, offers three Pete Dye-designed golf courses, 13 Har-Tru tennis courts, and the largest sporting clays facility in the hemisphere. *Info: Tel. 800/877-3643 or 809/523-3333, www.casadecampo.com.do.*

Puntacana Resort & Club $$$

Located on 105 acres with a three-mile beach, this expansive 420-room resort is just five minutes from the Punta Cana International Airport. Appealing to both adults and kids, the resort offers two golf courses, a spa, scuba diving, water skiing, sailing, fishing, windsurfing, and a full-service marina. *Info: Tel. 888/442-2262, www.puntacana.com.*

Iberostar Hacienda Dominicus $$

Located in Bayahibe, this expansive all-inclusive resort covers 30 acres of the Dominican Republic's tropical southern coast. All drinks, meals, and snacks are included in the cost, so you don't have to worry about watching the budget while on the island.

SLEEPS & EATS

SLEEPS & EATS

While at the Hacienda Dominicus, guests can try scuba diving, sunbathing at the pool, sailing on a catamaran, kayaking, and snorkeling. Land activities include billiards, volleyball, table tennis, and golf. Most visitors at this expansive resort arrive at nearby La Romana International Airport. From the airport, it's less than a half-hour drive to the resort, a drive past sugar cane fields and across the Chavon River, which served as a backdrop for *Apocolypse Now* and *Rambo 2*.

Pastel room blocks line the expansive pool complex. Walk from your room to the shade of a thatched palapa at poolside or head straight for the powdery white sand beach for the day. Active travelers can opt for snorkeling right offshore or sign up for a snorkeling or a dive trip. All nonmotorized watersports are included in the all-inclusive package.

Evening fun here is family-friendly with numerous restaurants from which to choose including Mexican, Japanese, and international. After dinner, most guests take in the evening show, an extravaganza on a scale that we've seen matched by few resorts in the Caribbean. And don't forget to have a look at the resident flamingos, who range freely in the fountains nearby. *Info: Tel. 888/923-2722 or 809/688-3600, www.iberostar.com.*

The Beach Club by Le Cirque $$
Located at Casa de Campo's private Minitas Beach, this casual lunch and dinner restaurant is the effort of the Maccioni family of New York's Le Cirque Restaurant. The restaurant features seafood, grilled meats,

SLEEPS & EATS

pasta, fresh salads and more, all overseen by Le Cirque-trained chefs. *Info: Casa de Campo, Tel. 809/523-3333.*

Meson de la Cava $$-$$$
Located in a cave (yes, a cave), this romantic setting is the perfect place to enjoy an intimate dinner. Specialties include grilled salmon filet in a maple and ginger sauce, cooked and served on a cedar plank, spinach lasagna, and Pechuga de Pollo, a grilled chicken breast in a tequila and lime marinade. Jackets are required in this restaurant, which is open daily. *Info: Av. Mirador Sur # 1, Santo Domingo, Tel. 809/533-2818 elmesondelacava.com.*

PRACTICAL MATTERS

Currency. The Dominican peso (RD) is the official currency. The exchange rate fluctuates but at press time was about RD $36 = $1 US.

Driving. Driving is on the right.

Electricity. 110 volt/60 cycles

Getting There. The Dominican Republic is home to numerous international airports so make sure you know the location of your resort before booking your air. On the south side of the island, the capital city of Santo Domingo is served by Las Americas International Airport, about a half-hour drive from the city. On the north side of the island, Puerto Plata is served by Puerto Plata International Gregorio Luperon Airport. Other airports include Punta

PRACTICAL MATTERS

Cana International Airport on the far east end, Maria Montez International Airport at Barahona, La Romana International Airport near Bavaro, and Arroyo Barril Airport in Samaná.

Information. For brochures on Dominican Republic attractions, call the Tourist Information Center, *Tel. 888/374-6361* in the US; *800/563-1611* in Canada.

Language. Spanish is the official language of the Dominican Republic. In tourist areas, English is spoken but away from the hotels you will need at least a minimal knowledge of Spanish.

Time. Atlantic Standard Time, one hour ahead of Eastern, is used throughout the year. Daylight savings time is not observed.

Website. *www.godominicanrepublic.com*

10. JAMAICA

For us, **Jamaica** means romance. Maybe it's the mountains covered in lush tropical vegetation. Maybe it's the plush resorts where couples are greeted by an atmosphere that promises pampering. Or maybe it's the people, who make visitors feel like they're returning home, a home where hummingbirds dart from bloom to bloom, where waters teeming with colorful marine life lie just steps from your room, where the island's own music makes nights pulsate with a tropical beat.

Jamaica was one of our first Caribbean destinations, and so, for us, a trip back to this island is indeed a homecoming. We try to make time for a meal at our favorite jerk joint. A stop by our favorite souvenir stand, a bamboo hut painted in Rastafarian colors. And, as we drive the sometimes bumpy roads filled with more-than-sometimes wild drivers, we pass by many of our favorite resorts and restaurants, and relive romantic times we've shared in Jamaica over the last decade.

INTRO

Jamaica, however, is not for everyone. Many travelers, including some fellow travel writers, prefer to skip this island because of the problems that inevitably reveal themselves even to the casual traveler. Drugs are a problem on this island, and you will probably be approached by ganja-selling entrepreneurs. Although the resorts patrol their grounds and beaches above the high water line, when you step outside the boundaries of the resort be prepared. "I have something special for you" is a frequently used line that you can ward off with a friendly but firm "No, thank you."

But, in general, we've found that Jamaica has some of the friendliest inhabitants in the Caribbean. Service, even in all-inclusive resorts where tips are not even a question, is unsurpassable. Taxi drivers are proud to tell you about the island, and we've even had drivers jump out of the car and pick (legal) herbs and plants along the route in describing their uses in the Jamaican household.

Jamaica's motto is "Out of Many, One People" and a quick look around the island confirms its multi-national history. The predominately African heritage has mixed with influences from South America, India, China, and Europe.

Jamaica's diversity comes from its visitors as well, guests from around the globe that make this tropical island home for a short while. Some of those visitors have become residents, most notably Errol Flynn, Ian Fleming, and Noel Coward. Flynn came to the island in the Forties and remained until his death in 1960, but not before he hit upon the idea of putting tourists on bamboo rafts on the Rio Grande, which today remains one of the most romantic rides in the Caribbean. Fleming, creator of the James Bond series, wrote from his home named "Goldeneye," located in Oracabessa near Ocho Rios. Today the home is owned by Chris Blackwell, founder of Island Records. At about the same period, Noel Coward arrived on the island, building a home named "Firefly" near Port Maria.

Licensed taxis are the best way for travelers to get around Jamaica. Even with recently improved roads on the north coast, traffic (on the left side of the road) is intense. Jamaica has one of the world's highest auto fatality rates. Rental cars are available but we'd suggest spending your first few days on the island in the care of a driver before you decide.

BEST SIGHTS IN JAMAICA

Because of the size of Jamaica, the sights you'll visit are somewhat limited by the resort area in which you're staying. Montego Bay has numerous attractions of its own but is within day trip distance of both Negril and Ocho Rios. Negril vacationers can squeeze in a trip to the South Coast or Montego Bay. Ocho Rios visitors can take a trip to Montego Bay or even Kingston. Port Antonio is pretty much a destination of its own.

Montego Bay

Several great houses, which once oversaw huge sugar plantations, are today notable visitor attractions. **Rose Hall**, *Tel. 876/953-2323*, is one of the best-known and is an easy afternoon visit for Montego Bay guests. This was once the home of the notorious Annie Palmer, better known as the White Witch. According to legend, Annie murdered several of her husbands and her slave lovers. Readers who would like to know more about the tales of Rose Hall can read the novel *The White Witch of Rose Hall*.

Jamaica may be the land of sun and fun but it's a birders' paradise as well. Bird lovers find one of the Caribbean's most unique sites at the **Rocklands Feeding Station**, *Tel. 876/952-2009*, in the village of Anchovy. This was the home of the late Lisa Salmon, Jamaica's best-known ornithologist. Her home is a veritable bird sanctuary surrounded by clouds of grassquits, saffron finches, and, most especially, hummingbirds.

From its location west of Montego Bay, **Chukka Caribbean Adventures**, *Tel. 876/953-5619*, *www.chukkacaribbean.com*, offers both biking and ATV tours. There's a minimum age

SIGHTS

of 16 on the ATV tours. The noisy ATVs jostle and splash their way along trails on a 10-mile ride through the hills before returning so visitors can take a dip in the sea. Also in Montego Bay, Chukka offers a popular canopy tour, allowing visitors to zipline high in the trees.

Negril & South Coast
Negril visitors don't have to venture all the way to Ocho Rios to enjoy waterfalls. Western Jamaica has a much quieter alternative in **Y.S. Falls**, *www.ysfalls.com*. These spectacular waterfalls cascade in steps through tropical forest. As spectacular (and far less crowded) as Dunn's River Falls, Y.S. is a Jamaican attraction that has remained untouched by hassling vendors and long lines. At the top, swimmers enjoy clear waters under a canopy of fern.

Nearby in the community of

Black River, enjoy the **Black River Safari Cruise**, *Tel. 876/965-2513*, a popular day trip for Negril vacationers looking for a little respite from sun and sand. This hour and a half long tour takes travelers up the Black River, at 44 miles the longest river in Jamaica. The waters here are home to snook and tarpon, some reaching as large as 200 pounds. You may see spear fishermen with a snorkel, mask and speargun, swimming in the dark water stained by peat deposits. The fisherman's canoes are hand-hewn and burned out using a generations-old technique. Among their catch are tiny brine shrimp, sold by women in the St. Elizabeth parish along the roadside. Highly salted and spiced, these are a popular snack with locals and visitors.

The biggest attraction on the Black River are the **crocodiles**. Once hunted, these crocodiles are now protected but still remain wary. These reptiles can live as long as 100 years, so long that some have become known by local residents.

SIGHTS

Ocho Rios

In Ocho Rios, the most popular attraction (one that just about every cruise ship passenger and resort guest enjoys—sometimes what seems like must be all at one time) is **Dunn's River Falls** (*see photo on page 101*). This spectacular waterfall is actually a series of falls that cascade from the mountains to the sea. Here you don't just view the falls, but you climb up the cascading water. Led by a sure-footed Jamaican guide, groups work their way up the falls hand-in-hand like a human daisy chain.

Be prepared to get wet and have fun, but don't expect a quiet, private getaway. This is Jamaica for the masses, and, no matter what day of the week, the masses do come. At the end of the climb, you'll be deposited into a hectic market for another opportunity to buy crafts, carvings, and the ubiquitous T-shirt.

Or would you like the chance to swim with dolphins? **Dolphin Cove at Treasure Reef**, *Tel. 876/974-5335, www.dolphincovejamaica.com*, near Dunn's River Falls, offers dolphin swims as well as lower-priced dolphin encounters, dolphin touch programs, or simple admission to the grounds, which also includes a short nature walk. Advance reservations are required.

Nearby stands one of Jamaica's newest (and one of our favorite) attractions: **Rainforest Bobsled Jamaica at Mystic Mountain**, *Tel. 876/974-3990*. You ride a chairlift up 700 feet above sea level where you can board Rainforest Bobsled Jamaica, a ride on steel rails through the rainforest.

The experience is good even for those who don't like fast rides; you have control of the brake yourself. Two riders can hook their bobsleds together. There's also a zipline canopy tour, lookout tower with a great view of Ocho Rios and the cruise port, and a 78-seat Caribbean restaurant.

Also in Ocho Rios, **Coyaba River Garden and Museum**,

SIGHTS

Shaw Park, *Tel. 876/974-2723*, is a good place to bring your young history buff. Exhibits start with pre-Columbian history and follow through the development of the island.

East of Ocho Rios in the town of Oracabessa, 007 fans can visit the **James Bond Beach**. Located near Ian Fleming's home, *Goldeneye*, the beach has plenty of options for a day of activity: waverunners, helicopter tours, stingray swim, and horseback rides as well as beach bar and grill.

Nearby, you'll find **Firefly**, once the home of playwright Noel Coward. Named for the luminous insects seen on the warm evenings, this house has certainly entertained its share of luminaries from the political and entertainment worlds including the Queen Mother, Laurence Olivier, Sophia Loren, Elizabeth Taylor, Alec Guiness, Peter O'Toole, and Richard Burton. Even today the house is kept in the same state it was when the Queen Mother came to lunch in 1965. A tour of Firefly includes a look at the home, photos of the house's many celebrity guests, and the grounds where Coward is now buried.

On the west side of Ocho Rios, check out the **Chukka Caribbean Adventures**, *Tel. 876/972-2506, www.chukkacaribbean.com*, between Runaway Bay and Ocho Rios. Well known for its world-class polo matches, the center also offers guided horseback trips along the beach and in the mountains. The polo horses were exercised in the sea, an activity the tourists saw and wanted to take part in so today visitors can ride on horseback right into the sea. You'll also find the **Jamaica Dogsled Experience** here with wheeled "sleds" pulled by former shelter dogs featured in a recent documentary, *Sun Dogs*.

BEST FESTIVAL
Celebrating summer, **Reggae Sumfest** is a week-long concert in July held in the Freeport area of Montego Bay. This event showcases talent that in the past has included Third World and Ziggy Marley and the Melody Makers. Tickets are sold for each night's performances or visitors can buy multi-event passes; you'll also find special hotel packages for the event. *Info: www.reggaesumfest.com*.

An excellent stop in Ocho Rios for travelers looking to get off the beaten path is **Cranbrook Flower Forest**, west of Ocho Rios at Laughlands, *Tel. 876/770-8071, www.cranbrookff.com*. This beautiful park, a recent addition to this area's tourist offerings, is a must-see for anyone who wants to experience the lush beauty away from the crowds. The park is the private creation of Ivan Linton, who has pampered the plants of this former plantation for over two decades.

BEST SHOPPING

This island has a wealth of **arts and crafts**, everything from colorful paintings to folk art wood carvings, not to mention batik T-shirts and crocheted tams in Rastafarian colors (yellow, red and green). Shopping at the roadside stands or on the beach involves negotiating the price. It's part of the fun.

Our favorite purchases are the **woodcarvings**, both freestanding and bas relief of local animal life, faces, fish, and just about everything else you can imagine. The finest pieces are carved from lignum vitae, or wood of life, a pale hardwood that is so dense it won't float. If you get a woodcarving, don't forget to ask the artist to sign it for you. The craftsmen have great pride in their work and most are happy to oblige.

Montego Bay is also home of the **Craft Market**. Many travelers avoid the market because of fears of high-pressure sales, but we have found the market delightful. A friendly "good morning," abstaining from photos until a purchase (no matter how small) is made, and general good manners will go far with the salespeople. On a recent visit, one cheerful vendor gave us a small basket as a gift. After shopping, take a break with a soft drink or "sky juice" (like our snow cone) sold from pushcarts beneath the shade trees.

For fixed prices, head to the **shopping centers**. East of Montego Bay in the Rose Hall area (nicknamed the Elegant Corridor for its high-end resorts and shopping), the top shopping centers are The

SHOPPING

SHOPPING

Shoppes at Rose Hall and the Half Moon Shopping Village. In Negril, Time Square is home of the community's most serious shopping. Ocho Rios is home to the Taj Mahal Shopping Centre, a complex of fine duty-free shops and other stores that sell souvenir items, and Blue Mountain coffee.

In every resort area, be prepared for numerous offers by higglers, Jamaica's word for peddlers. Also be prepared for offers of "something spe-cial." *Ganja* or marijuana is widespread, but purchase or use of the drug is strictly illegal.

A very legal agricultural product is **Jamaican Blue Mountain coffee**, considered one of the finest coffees in the world. Gift shops at the resorts and the airport sell the coffee in small burlap gift bags for about $1 US per ounce (less than half the price found in American coffee shops). You can find the coffee even cheaper at local markets.

BEST SPORTS & RECREATION

Each resort area has plenty of snorkeling and diving options. Except for Port Antonio, each also has golf; golfers will find that Jamaica is one of the Caribbean's top golf destinations with plenty of challenges and beautiful courses that take advantage of both the island's rolling terrain and seaside views. You'll find dazzling courses across the island, from the best known fairways in the Montego Bay area to lovely courses in Ocho Rios, Runaway Bay, Negril, Kingston, and Mandeville. The top courses on the island are Tryall, White Witch (*photo at left*), and Half Moon, all in the Montego Bay area. Wherever you play, use of a caddy is mandatory.

SPORTS & RECREATION

SLEEPS & EATS

BEST SLEEPS & EATS

Jamaica has a wide assortment of accommodations. The island is especially known for its all-inclusive resorts including many for adults only. You'll also find traditional hotels, numerous villas, and small inns across the island.

KINGSTON
Strawberry Hill $$$$
Far from the madding beach resorts, Strawberry Hill promises sophisticated simplicity deeply in tune with restorative nature. The curative powers of the place have drawn many visitors over the years but none more famous than reggae superstar and Jamaica national hero Bob Marley. In 1976, Marley sought the tranquility of Strawberry Hill while recuperating from a gunshot

wound. The resort was owned (and still is) by Chris Blackwell, Marley's music producer. Marley may be Strawberry Hill's most famous guest but he's by no means the only notable name in the hotel registry. Mick Jagger, Melissa Manchester, Robert Palmer and, during our stay, models Kate Moss and Naomi Campbell were guests for a few days respite from the lime-light.

Strawberry Hill is composed of villas, each filled with antique Jamaican decor. The villas survey the Blue Mountains from bedrooms, living rooms, and expansive porches. Every room includes electric mattress pads to warm up the bed on chilly evenings, mosquito-netted mahogany four-poster beds, stocked kitchenettes, and more. An Aveda spa ensures a relaxing stay. *Info: Tel. 800/OUTPOST (US and Canada), 876/944-8400, www.islandoutpost.com/strawberry_hill.*

SLEEPS & EATS

MONTEGO BAY
Half Moon $$$-$$$$

Half Moon is one of Jamaica's top destination resorts, a place you can check into and be perfectly happy until you're ready to depart. In fact, there's no reason not to be: facilities here include a shopping village, hospital, school, dolphin swims, a golf course, and equestrian center. What started out in 1954 as a group of private beach cottages offered for rent during off-season months has blossomed into one of Jamaica's most extensive resorts.

Those beach cottages are still available and—just steps away from the sand as well as public areas— remain a great choice. We stayed in the cottages on our last stay and loved the easy proximity both to the public areas and to the beach. Some accommodations are a long walk from public areas although a call can arrange for a golf cart pickup. The villas come with a private golf cart for your use.

Half Moon is the Caribbean's only resort with a private dolphin experience. The Dolphin Lagoon is home to four dolphins available for swims and encounters with resort guests only. The resort recently opened the new 68,000-square-foot Fern Tree Spa and six beachfront spa suites. The project follows the renovation of the resort's Robert Trent Jones Sr.-designed golf course, the beachfront Hibiscus and the Oleander deluxe suites, two restaurants, and more, all part of a five-year master plan. *Info: Tel. 888/830-5974 or 876/953–2211, www.halfmoon.com.*

Ritz-Carlton Golf & Spa Resort Rose Hall, Jamaica $$$$
If you're looking for luxury, you'll be, well, putting on the Ritz at this elegant resort located east of Montego Bay. A favorite with

golfers thanks to its lauded White Witch Golf Course (located on the grounds of the historic Rose Hall Great House), the resort has a beachfront location and the  highbrow service for which the Ritz is known. This resort is the only one of all the Ritz-Carlton resorts that offers an optional all-inclusive plan. *Info: Tel. 800/241-3333 or 876/953-2800, www.ritzcarlton.com.*

Round Hill Hotel & Villas $$$$

A favorite of the rich and famous set, Round Hill offers suites, traditional hotel rooms and 27 villas. Expensive and lavish, the villas include maid service (cook service is available as well), and many have a private pool. The resort includes numerous amenities, from tennis courts to a dive shop to windsurfing. If you check out the website and Round Hill looks familiar, there's a good reason: the property was the location of many scenes in *How Stella Got Her Groove Back. Info: Tel. 800/972-2159 (US) or 876/956-7050, www.roundhilljamaica.com.*

Sandals Royal Caribbean Resort & Private Island $$$-$$$$

A quieter option than Sandals Montego Bay and more upscale than Sandals Inn, Sandals Royal Caribbean is one of our favorite Sandals properties and includes a large resort as well as a private island. Sandals Cay, reached by a "dragon boat" serves as a sunbathing setting in the daytime and romantic restaurant location at night. On land, the resort has numerous room categories including swim-up River Suites. Some room categories include butler service. *Info: Tel. 800/SANDALS, 876/953–2231, www.sandals.com.*

SLEEPS & EATS

The Tryall Club $$$$

If you're a golfer, you're probably already familiar with Tryall, a celebrity resort that has hosted many tournament games and is considered one of the Caribbean's best golf courses. This posh getaway includes everything you need to hole up and never leave, if you so choose. Along with the course, the resort features private villas with their own pools, tennis courts, dive shops, a driving range and more. You'll never feel crowded at this 2,200-acre property. *Info: Tel. 800/238-5290 or 876/975-0269, www.tryallclub.com.*

NEGRIL
The Caves $$$$

At this tranquil property, part of the exclusive Island Outpost group, guests fall asleep to the sound of waves echoing through the namesake for this inn, sea caves formed from ancient volcanic rock and the pounding surf. In the day, vacationers leave one of the hand-crafted, thatched-roofed cottages and snorkel among these grottos and caves or sun on the decks among the cliffs. The Caves offers Aveda spa services, from massage to an invigorating sea salt glow using salts from the Dead Sea. Breakfast and lunch are served beneath a thatched palapa and dinner is available by arrangement. The Caves also has a saltwater plunge pool and cliffside Jacuzzi. Rooms are decorated with hand-carved furniture and center around a bed draped in mosquito netting. *Info: Tel. 800/OUTPOST (US and Canada) or 876/960-8134, www.islandoutpost.com/the_caves.*

Couples Swept Away Negril $$-$$$

Couples Swept Away is a favorite with active couples thanks to its 10-acre sports complex. The facility includes squash, tennis, racquetball, basketball, a lap pool, jogging track, gym, and more. Of special interest to tennis lovers in the fall months, Couples Swept Away features world-class tennis with pros from across the US offering tips and classes.

Travelers can also explore the region on complimentary off-site excursions including golf at Negril Hills Golf Club (greens fees and transfers are complimentary but required caddy fees are not

SLEEPS & EATS

included), a sunset catamaran cruise, or a trip to a local sunset bar.

Every September, the resort celebrates Spa and Wellness month with special programs and classes free for guests. Options ranging from programs on medical hypnosis to herbal treatments are planned for the annual month-long event. *Info: Tel. 800/268-7537, 876/957-4061, www.couples.com.*

Rockhouse $$
Just steps from West End Road, once through the gates at Rockhouse you'll feel that you are tucked away from the world. The restaurant and bar are perched high on Negril's bluffs and look directly out to sea and an unbeatable sunset. Rooms here are constructed from wood, thatch and stone with a natural theme carried out in the open-air showers. If your budget won't allow you a stay at The Caves, Rockhouse makes a great alternative at a far lower price. *Info: Tel. 876/957-4373, www.rockhousehotel.com.*

OCHO RIOS
Couples Tower Isle $$$-$$$$
Recently renovated, this all-inclusive (formerly Couples Ocho Rios) sports an all-new look with a South Beach meets Rat Pack vibe that harkens back to the resort's 1940s roots. Couples has a large white sand beach with a full menu of watersports. If you want an all-over tan, a boat will carry you out to a small island specially set aside for nude sunbathing, where you can enjoy plenty of sun as well as a dip in the pool and a cocktail at the swim-up bar. *Info: Tel. 800/268-7537, 876/975-4271, www.couples.com.*

Goldeneye $$$$

If you're a Bond buff wondering where to stay on your next visit to Jamaica, this might just be the place. Located eight minutes from Oracabessa (15 minutes from Ochi), Goldeneye is a one-of-a-kind getaway. Goldeneye was the Jamaica home of author Ian Fleming and here, at his modest desk, each of the 007 novels were penned. Today that original Goldeneye home is the Ian Fleming Villa, a three-bedroom accommodation with a garden dining area, private beach and full-time staff to whip up meals. The property also includes cottages, each with indoor and outdoor dining facilities, kitchen, private beach access and entertainment/TV room. In 2010, Goldeneye closes its doors to expand and will reopen later in the year. *Info: Tel. 800/OUT-POST, www.islandoutpost.com/goldeneye.*

Jamaica Inn $$$$

This classic Caribbean inn with 45 suites has drawn such visitors as model Kate Moss, Phil Donahue, Marlo Thomas and actor  Albert Finney. Sir Winston Churchill was a frequent guest here and favored the White Suite. Each suite has a beach view, private verandah and antique furnishings. The inn is also home to a noted restaurant. A clifftop spa offers ayurveda treatments. *Info: Tel. 800/837-4608 or 876/974-2514, www.jamaicainn.com.*

Royal Plantation Ocho Rios, Jamaica $$$$

Dating back to the Fifties, this elegant hideaway, styled like an old plantation mansion, was used in the filming of *Prelude to a Kiss*, starring Meg Ryan and Alec Baldwin. Although today the resort is owned by Butch Stewart of Sandals fame, this boutique property is not an all-inclusive and maintains a more exclusive atmosphere than its siblings. The hotel is perched high on a bluff and is known for its personal service and fine dining; optional butler service is available. *Info: Tel. 888/48-ROYAL or 876/974-5601, www.royalplantation.com.*

SLEEPS & EATS

RUNAWAY BAY

Breezes Runaway Bay $$

This property was one of our first stops when we came to the island. At that time, it was known as Jamaica-Jamaica. The property, still part of the SuperClubs chain, has seen many renovations and is still one of the most popular resorts on the island. Guests here enjoy complimentary use of a golf course and school right across the road, as well as tennis, horseback riding, windsurfing and more. Rooms have a tropical decor and the grounds are always immaculate (as with all SuperClubs). *Info: Tel. 877/GO-SUPER or 876/973-6099, www.superclubs.com.*

SOUTH COAST

Jake's $-$$$

In the past few years, Jake's has almost become synonymous with Treasure Beach and, while small, is a top name on the South Coast. Part of Island Outpost, Jake's is a unique property, a place for those really looking to get away from it all and into a relaxed rhythm with the sea.

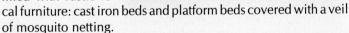

Beach kitsch best describes the decor of the resort's eight guest units, each in pale shades of ochre, blue, pink and lavender with tin roofs. Each of the guest rooms at Jake's is filled with rustic local furniture: cast iron beds and platform beds covered with a veil of mosquito netting.

The co-owner of Jake's, Jason Henzell, is also involved in an important community program on the South Coast called Breds. Established by Henzell and Peace Corps volunteer Aaron Laufer in 1998, Breds (short for Brethren, a term often used by local residents to greet each other) is a non-profit association that promotes education, sports, cultural heritage, and environmental awareness.

SLEEPS & EATS

Some Breds projects have included the construction of 30 local houses in the Treasure Beach community; hosting 14 New York City doctors to train local volunteers to be first responders; donation of fishing boats to needy residents; the completion of an expansion to the local primary school; adding a computer lab and library, and more. *Info: Tel. 800/OUTPOST (US and Canada), 876/965-3000, www.islandoutpost.com/jakes.*

Sandals Whitehouse European Village & Spa $$$-$$$$

The newest Sandals resort in Jamaica is also the island's most unique. This property is, like the others, a couples-only property but here, like the rest of the South Coast, exploration of the region is especially encouraged. During our stay, we visited many sites in the area ranging from side of the road eateries to local attractions. The resort is constructed in European-style "villages" with Dutch, French and Italian styles. The room blocks stretch along the beachfront so no rooms are too far from the sands. Public areas are found in a central "village" with sidewalk bistros, a strolling violinist and a very pleasurable atmosphere. *Info: Tel. 888/SANDALS or 867/957-5216, www.sandals.com.*

JAMAICAN CUISINE

Jamaica's motto is "Out of Many, One People" and it's a saying that could equally be applied to the island's food. Residents have come from around the globe, bringing with them the cooking techniques, flavors, spices, and recipes of their homelands and blending them with the bountiful harvest of this tropical island. One of the most famous dishes on the island is **jerk**. This Jamaican barbecue originated in the 1930s along Boston Beach, east of Port Antonio. Here the first roadside (or wayside) stands sprang up offering tasty jerk served in a super casual atmosphere. Today jerk stands are everywhere on the island but many aficionados still return to Boston Beach for the "real thing."

The meat—pork, chicken, or fish—is marinated with a fiery mixture of spices including Scotch bonnet peppers, pimento (called allspice elsewhere), nutmeg, escallion, and thyme. It's all served with even more hot sauce, a rice and bean dish known as rice and peas, and a wonderful bread called festival.

Evita's Italian Restaurant $$

This longtime favorite is patronized by travelers and locals alike for good Italian fare. Perched high over the city in a house more than a century old, Evita's is especially noted for its numerous pasta and seafood dishes. Menu selections include homemade fettuccine with meat sauce; fettuccine Alfredo; and red snapper fillet stuffed with crab meat and jumbo shrimp sautéed in garlic butter, white wine and tomatoes. *Info: Eden Bower Rd., Ocho Rios, Tel. 876/974–2333.*

The Pork Pit $

Jerk chicken, spare ribs, steam roast fish, sweet potatoes, roast yam, festival and cold coconut water star at this fast-food eatery that's a favorite with locals, located across from Walter Fletcher Beach. Order up a plate and then grab a place at one of the picnic tables on the patio. Like the menu here, seating is simple with no frills. This is one of the top places in Montego Bay for traditional island jerk. *Info: Gloucester Avenue, Montego Bay, Tel. 876/940-3008.*

Scotchies $

One of our favorite jerk stops, this Montego Bay tradition is casual, fun and inexpensive. The open-air eatery offers plates of jerk chicken, sausage, pork, and ribs, all accompanied by *festival* (a rolled bread similar to a Southern hush puppy), *bammy* (fried cassava bread), and some fire-breathing hot sauce. In Ocho Rios, visit Scotchie's Too, located at Drax Hall. *Info: Coral Gardens (North Coast Highway near Holiday Inn), Montego Bay, Tel. 876/953-3301.*

Strawberry Hill $$-$$$

Located at the hotel by the same name, this restaurant has an open terrace with an unbeatable view of Kingston on clear days. The restaurant features "new Jamaican cuisine" in dishes such as Jerked Lamb Loin with a Road Garlic Guava Glaze, Mashed Potatoes and Green Plantations, Pan Seared Herb Crusted Grouper Filet with a Chive Mushroom Nage, and Coconut Curried shrimp bring new twists to traditional island food. Reservations needed. *Info: Strawberry Hill, New Castle Road, Irishtown, Tel. 876/ 944-8400 .*

PRACTICAL MATTERS

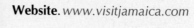

Currency. The Jamaican dollar is the official tender; its exchange rate fluctuates frequently but at press time was about $1 US = $89J. US dollars are accepted throughout the island.

Driving. Driving is British style, on the left.

Electricity. 110volts/50 cycles (although 220 is used in some hotels)

Getting There. Jamaica has two major international airports located in Montego Bay and Kingston, the capital city. Most travelers, whether headed to Montego Bay, Negril, Ocho Rios, Runaway Bay or the South Coast, fly into Montego Bay. Port Antonio travelers fly into Kingston.

Information. Jamaica Tourist Board, *Tel. 800/233-4JTB*.

Language. English is the official language, although you'll frequently hear the Jamaican patois on the street, a combination of several languages.

Time. Jamaica is on Eastern Standard Time and does not observe Daylight Savings Time.

Website. *www.visitjamaica.com*

11. PUERTO RICO

Ready for a fiesta? Then set your course on **Puerto Rico**. Here, in the capital city of San Juan, you'll find a pulsating atmosphere that can't be topped anywhere in the Caribbean. Casinos ring with the clink of slots; showgirls kick up their heels in lavish revues; couples jump out on the dance floor and shake to the sounds of salsa and merengue.

But beyond the boundaries of San Juan, the sounds change to the slap of waves on the honey-colored shore or the peeping of the tiny coqui (co-kee), a frog that's a national symbol of Puerto Rico. (It's said that the coqui can survive only on the island, so to be "as Puerto Rican as a coqui" is a declaration of island pride.)

INTRO

Puerto Rico is an easy destination to like. It's simple to reach—just 2-1/2 hours from Miami and under four hours from New York; there's a wide variety of attractions no matter what your interest; it's still in the United States while at the same time offering all the intrigue of a foreign destination.

Your first introduction to Puerto Rico will probably be arrival in **San Juan**. This high-rise city hugs the coastline like a Caribbean version of Miami (but with casinos) and offers all the amenities you'd expect in a metropolitan area this size. It's so large that it's divided into several districts. Travelers typically visit Condado, Isla Verde, and Old San Juan, the historical heart of the city. Here you'll find buildings so old and quaint they look more like part of a movie set than part of a modern downtown district.

The historical heart of the city is **Old San Juan**, home of the best known sites including **Fuerte San Felipe del Morro** or El Morro (*photo below*). This fort, one of the most photographed places in the Caribbean, is administered by the U.S. National Park Service. You can take a self-guided tour; exhibit signs are posted in both English and Spanish. Even if you're not a history buff, El Morro is a great place to gaze out on the sea and enjoy the gentle tradewinds. Don't miss the "garitas," circular sentry towers now a symbol of Puerto Rico.

But for all its historic and city attractions, San Juan is still a beach town. Along the water's edge of **Isla Verde Beach**, you'll see surfers and swimmers frol-

icking in the waves, seemingly oblivious to the urban scene just beyond the sand. Nature also takes center stage at **El Yunque National Forest**, the only tropical rainforest in the US National Forest Service. Forty-five minutes east of San Juan, the rainforest blooms with 240 species of trees, ferns, and flowers. Walking trails wind through the dense forest, and **La Mina Falls** (*photo at right*) is well worth your time.

After dinner, the action lies in the city's casinos, most remaining open until the early hours of the morning. You'll find a full menu of table games and slots at the **luxury hotels in the Condado and Isla Verde districts**. Formerly, these casinos required jackets but today the dress code is semi-formal, just no shorts and sneakers.

Beyond San Juan, the city gives way to a beautiful countryside rich with agriculture, over 200 miles of coastline, and a spirit that welcomes visitors with a hearty "Buenos dias."

Mountains form a rugged ridge from east to west. These mountains, the Cordillera Central and the Sierra de Luquillo, loom at about 3000 feet above sea level and ease into rolling hills before reaching the coastal plains. The rainiest area is in the northeastern mountains in the El Yunque rain forest, an area rich with tropical lushness ranging from breadfruit to mahogany trees to orchids. Puerto Rico's southwestern side sports cacti and succulents as it receives only a fraction of the rain forest's total precipitation.

Rincón, on the island's northwestern end, is the surfing capital of the Caribbean. From January through April, those surfers are joined by migratory humpback whales, so even if you're not ready to hang ten the two of you can head out from Rincón on a whale watching excursion. Off Puerto Rico's shores, **the islands of Mona, Culebra, and Vieques** offer quiet getaways for those willing to take an extra hop.

Rental cars from the major US agencies are available, especially in the San Juan area. Driving is on the right and signage is bilingual. However, realize that San Juan is a major metropolitan area and just as difficult to maneuver as any other city its size. The Old San Juan area is especially congested, with old, narrow streets.

Taxis are a popular choice, especially within San Juan. A **Taxi Turisticos** program sets specified rates within certain zones and are an excellent choice for first-time visitors. These taxis are white and bear the words Taxi Turisticos and a drawing of El Morro. The drivers have received special training to serve the tourist zones.

BEST SIGHTS IN PUERTO RICO

Old San Juan is dotted with museums and historic sites. The best known is **Fuerte San Felipe del Morro** or **El Morro,** *Old San Juan, Tel. 787/729-6777.* This fort, one of the most photographed sites in the Caribbean, contains a museum and is administered by the National Park Service. On its grounds, the Cuartel de Ballaja, once Spanish troop quarters, now houses the Museum of the Americas. You'll find a map at the entrances, and exhibits throughout the park are posted in both English and Spanish. Even if you're not a history buff, this site is a place where you can look out on the sea and enjoy a gentle tradewind. Bring along your camera for this scenic stop.

Nearby, **Casa Blanca,** *1*

Sebastian Street, Old San Juan, contains exhibits on 16th and 17th century life and on its most famous residents: Ponce de Leon and his family. (Actually Ponce de Leon died before the home was completed.) Built in the 1520s, the home was the city's first fortress and is now open for tours.

Puerto Rico is also rich in natural attractions, including one of the finest cave systems in the world. The **Rio Camuy Cave Park**, *Route 102, Tel. 787/898-3100*, located 2-1/2 hours west of San Juan, was formed by large underground rivers. Today the park includes a new visitors center with reception area and cafeteria and a theater with AV presentation. Visitors reach cave level by trolley then follow walk-

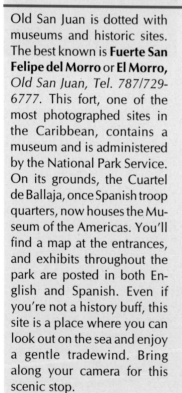

ways on a 45-minute guided tour.

Another natural attraction is **El Yunque National Forest**, Highway 3 east between San Juan and Fajardo to Route 191 near Luquillo, *Tel. 787/888-1810*, the only tropical rainforest in the US National Forest Service. Forty-five minutes east of San Juan, the rainforest boasts 240 species of trees and flowers, including 20 varieties of orchids and 50 varieties of ferns. Walking trails carve through the dense forest, and guided tours are available.

One of our favorite excursions is a snorkel trip out to **Monkey Island**. More fun than a barrel of monkeys, this island of curious primates is located off the southeast coast of Puerto Rico. It's a sanctuary for hundreds of monkeys, and access to the island is prohibited. Visitors cannot actually step on land, but you can snorkel around the fringes of the island while excited primates hoot and holler at the intrusion. We found the snorkeling here excellent as well, full of colorful fans and bright corals.

CASINOS

Casino gambling is found at many hotels. Most casinos open at noon and remain open until the early hours of the morning. Most have dress codes which require semi-formal attire; leave the shorts, tank tops, and flip-flops in the room for your night at the tables. This is your chance to dress up and party; with San Juan's lively atmosphere the rule of thumb is the tighter, the shinier, the better. You may be surprised to learn that alcohol cannot, by law, be served in Puerto Rico's casinos. You will find bars in each hotel, but no drinks are served on the casino floor.

One of the most sophisticated casinos in San Juan, and, indeed in the Caribbean, is found at **El San Juan Hotel**. With a tuxedoed staff and an elegant European air, it's a favorite for couples looking for a fine casino.

El Conquistador offers a large casino with a view of the sea (yes—windows in a casino!) The entire casino is well-lit and bright, with pale paneling, beautiful views, and an airy atmosphere.

Baseball buffs are in the right place. Watch major league stars during the Winter League, from November through January. The games take place nearly nightly in San Juan's Hiram Bithorn Stadium and tickets are just $6 and under.

BEST FESTIVAL

Held in late May, the four-day **Heineken JazzFest** draws some of the top names in the jazz world as well as many travelers. Now two decades old, the event is held at San Juan's Tito Puente Amphitheater. *Info: www.prheinekenjazz.com.*

BEST SHOPPING

Shopping is a major activity for Puerto Rico visitors. Duty-free shopping is found at the Luis Muñoz Marin International Airport and at factory outlet shops in **Old San Juan**. If you're looking for gold and jewelry or factory outlets, check out the shops on **Calle Christo** and **Calle Fortaleza** in Old San Juan.

If you're homesick for an American mall, head over to **Plaza Las Americas**, which claims to be the largest shopping center in the Caribbean. Here you'll find over 300 shops with everything from designer clothes to fine art to fine jewelry. The mall is located in the Hato Rey region, the main business district in San Juan.

If you're looking for an island product, popular purchases are *cuatros* (small handmade guitars), *mundillo* (bobbin lace), *santos* (hand carved religious figures), rum, and cigars.

BEST SLEEPS & EATS

Unlike other Caribbean islands, you won't find all-inclusive resorts in Puerto Rico. You will find some of the region's most expansive properties with a full menu of on-site activities. Spa and golf are strong points in Puerto Rico.

El San Juan Hotel & Casino $$$-$$$$

El San Juan is a convenient and luxurious hotel that's just minutes from the airport. Fresh from a renovation of its 382 guest rooms, the hotel is now part of the Waldorf Astoria Collection. This hotel could symbolize the elegance of San Juan. A lobby paneled in rich woods greets visitors, and just steps away the most elegant casino in the Caribbean offers games of chance managed by croupiers in black tie. The pool area is beautifully landscaped with tropical gardens, the perfect place to relax after a morning of touring or shopping in San Juan. *Info: Tel. 888/579-2632, 787/791-1000, www.elsanjuanhotel.com.*

El Conquistador Resort & Golden Door Spa $$$$

Now part of the Waldorf Astoria Collection, El Conquistador stands perched atop a 300-foot cliff and ranks as one of the grandest resorts in the region. With 984  guest rooms, it's not the place for those looking for privacy and to get away from the crowds, but you'll find just about everything else at this luxury resort. Choose from an 18-hole championship golf course, a private marina with rental boats and charters for deep-sea fishing, scuba facilities, seven swimming pools, seven tennis courts, a nightclub, casino, fitness center, salon, and luxurious shops—not to mention a 100-acre private island, Palomina, reached via complimentary ferry. On secluded Palomina, enjoy snorkeling, nature trails, and siestas in hammocks stretched between tall palms. *Info: Tel. 888/543-1282, www.elconresort.com.*

SLEEPS & EATS

Grand Melia Puerto Rico Resort $$$$

This resort was built as Puerto Rico's first all-inclusive resort—but soon changed to a European Plan resort. Here 486 suites, all

housed in low-rise, two-story buildings, offer beachside relaxation. And for pampering with plenty of elbow room, there are five garden villas, 12 honeymoon suites and a Presidential Suite with its own swimming pool. Puerto Rico is well-known for its golf courses, and this property fits right into the island's offerings thanks to its neighboring Coco Beach Golf and Country Club. The clubhouse has a lawn with views of El Yunque rainforest. Two championship courses designed by Tom Kite and Bruce Besse offer special greens fees for resort guests as well as preferred tee times, private lessons and storage of clubs. Landlubbers find plenty of other diversions on property: volleyball, table tennis, tennis, bicycles, billiards and more. *Info: Tel. 888/95-MELIA, 787/809-1770, www.gran-melia-puerto-rico.com.*

Rio Mar Beach Resort & Spa, A Wyndham Grand Resort $$$-$$$$

Fresh from a $40 million capital improvement project, this 627-room resort offers a 7,000-square-foot casino, two 18-hole golf

courses designed by Tom and George Fazio and Greg Norman, a 7,000-square-foot spa and fitness center, 11 restaurants, an international tennis center and more. *Info: Tel. 787/888-6000, www.wyndhamriomar.com.*

The Villas at Palmas $$$$

For vacationers looking to get away from the glitz of San Juan, the Villas at Palmas is an excellent choice. Located 45 minutes from the capital city, the resort lies tucked on the Caribbean side of the island near the town of Humacao. Actually a collection of several resorts that range from standard hotel rooms to a bed and breakfast inn to luxury condominiums, Palmas is a city in itself with a staff of over 500 employees.

Although three and a half miles of groomed beach (plus another six miles of nearly deserted beach) tempt vacationers to soak up sun and surf, the sports facilities offer plenty of opportunities to stay busy. The Golf Club features two championship courses with holes offering views of El Yunque rain forest, the sea, and the nearby island of Vieques. The largest tennis center in the Caribbean has classes for players of every level. *Info: Tel. 800/468-3331; www.villasatpalmas.com/reservations.htm.*

La Mallorquina $$$

Since 1848, this casual eatery in Old San Juan has offered fine Puerto Rican cuisine: paella, fried rice with shrimp, chicken *asopao*, and even Puerto Rican-style beef tenderloin. *Info: Calle San Justo 207, Old San Juan, Tel. 787/722-3261.*

PUERTO RICAN CUISINE

Meals in Puerto Rico are late and lengthy. In San Juan, the trendiest area for fine dining followed by an evening of bar hopping is "**Sofo**," the South Fortaleza district. Look for restaurants featuring "Nuevo Latino Cuisine" as well as traditional *Criolla* or Puerto Rican dishes, a mix of Taíno, Spanish and African influences. Start with an appetizer of *tostones* (fried plantains) before moving on to *asopao* (rice and chicken stew) and *mofongo* (seasoned mashed plantains). Save room for *tembleque*, a custard made with coconut milk and sprinkled with cinnamon. And there's no need to worry about going thirsty: along with some of the Caribbean's finest rums, the island offers excellent local beer and stout Puerto Rican coffee.

La Dorada $$-$$$

Puerto Rican cuisine is also the specialty of this casual restaurant that features many seafood dishes. Choose from broiled halibut, red snapper in lobster and shrimp sauce, rice with squid, lobster *asopao*, or *mofongo* stuffed with seafood. *Info: 1105 Ave. Magdalena, Condado, Tel. 787/722-9583.*

The Parrot Club $$-$$$

This fun restaurant has a tropical courtyard and a definite Caribbean feel. The menu features a wide array of Latino dishes with a twist, from ceviche to blackened tuna. *Info: The Parrot Club363 Fortaleza St., Old San Juan, Tel. 787/725-7370*

PRACTICAL MATTERS

Currency. The US dollar is the official currency.

Driving. Driving is on the right side. Most road signs are in both English and Spanish.

Electricity. The island uses 110 volts, 60 cycles.

Getting There. Puerto Rico boasts excellent air service via the Luis Muñoz Marin International Airport in San Juan.

Language. Both Spanish and English are the official languages of Puerto Rico. You'll find plenty of English spoken in the resort areas and in San Juan but in the smaller communities most conversation is in Spanish.

Information. Puerto Rico Tourism Company, *Tel. 800/866-7827* in US, *800/667-0394* in Canada.

Time. Puerto Rico is located in the Atlantic Time Zone, one hour ahead of Eastern. The island does not observe Daylight Savings Time.

Website. *www.gotopuertorico.com.*

12. ST. KITTS AND NEVIS

Imagine a country inn where rooms brim with antiques and are cooled by a gentle breeze off a wide porch. You ease into a wicker chair, sip an icy drink, and enjoy a view unbroken by roads, electrical lines, or even fellow travelers.

This is **St. Kitts and Nevis**, partners in a Caribbean two-island nation that offers all the country comfort and bed-and-breakfast luxury you might look for in a New England getaway. Here, however, palms replace pines and color comes, not from scarlet leaves, but from azure seas, beaches in shades of both black and white, and verdant forests that cloak the islands.

INTRO

St. Kitts and Nevis boast one of the Caribbean's largest concentrations of plantation homes. The islands were once dotted with sugar plantations and greathouses, but today these stately manses have been transformed into elegant bed-and-breakfast inns especially popular with European vacationers and with Americans looking to experience a slice of the Caribbean "the way it used to be." Don't expect reggae lessons, limbo contests or mixology classes at these properties; instead, you will find a sophisticated atmosphere where the emphasis lies, not on providing fun for its guests, but in pointing the way for independent travelers to make their own discoveries.

St. Kitts and Nevis are both mountainous by Caribbean standards and rich with undeveloped regions. Both islands are home to small rain forests, although visitors will find plenty of tropical foliage wherever they venture.

Shaped like a guitar, **St. Kitts** is the more developed of the two. Most of its 35,000 residents live in the town of **Basseterre** (pronounced bos-tear) on the south shore (just where the guitar handle meets the body.)

South of Basseterre, the island slims, the land becomes drier, and the population scattered. This is the **South Peninsula**, an area that, until a few years ago, was accessible only by boat. Today a modern highway makes this region available to motorists. Here you'll find some of the island's most **beautiful, remote beaches** and roadside overlooks with views of both sides of the island and the Caribbean Sea to the south and the Atlantic Ocean to the north. Animal lovers, the South Peninsula is your best chance for spotting **vervet monkeys**. Look in the underbrush and not in the trees, however. These monkeys don't have a prehensile tail so are usually spotted on the ground.

The north end of St. Kitts is the most lush, due to soil that owes its fertility to a volcano named **Mount Liamuiga**, a Carib word that means "fertile island." The remote reaches of Mount Liamuiga are covered by rain forest. *See photo on page 141.*

For all the tropical splendor of St. Kitts, **Nevis** is even more verdant. Tall coconut palms cover hills carpeted in tropical undergrowth. Covering a total of just 36 square miles, this small island was first named Santa Maria de las Nieves by Columbus because of the ever-present cloud that give **Mount Nevis** a snow-capped look. Home to only 9,000 residents, this country cousin has a charming atmosphere all its own, plus a good share of plantation houses with period antiques and wide breezy porches.

Getting around either St. Kitts or Nevis is simple but will involve either a taxi (a good choice for your first day) or a rental car (a good choice if you're in one of the more remote plantation inns.) Traffic on Nevis is especially light (although signage is poor in some areas...but what a great place to get lost!)

BEST SIGHTS IN ST. KITTS AND NEVIS

SIGHTS

St. Kitts

More fun than a barrel of monkeys, St. Kitts tempts travelers with days of sightseeing. Budget a day for an overall look at the sights, which range from historic homes and museums to natural formations and Indian petroglyphs.

The most recognized feature on St. Kitts is **Brimstone Hill Fortress National Park** (*photo at right*) one of the top historical attractions in the Caribbean. From over 800 feet above sea level, you'll enjoy one of the best views found on any of the islands. On a clear day, you can see Nevis, Montserrat, Saba, St. Martin, and St. Barts.

Brimstone Hill, nicknamed "The Gibraltar of the West Indies," is one of the largest forts in the islands. A mandatory stop for anyone interested in military history, the volcanic stone structure took more than a century to construct and is named for the faint sulfur smell, a legacy of the volcano, sometimes encountered here.

SIGHTS

Travelers who want to learn more about the history of the island can jump aboard the **St. Kitts Scenic Railway National Tour**. The train chugs across the island on the track that was built in 1912 to deliver sugar cane from the plantations to the sugar mill in Basseterre. It has been in constant agricultural operation since then.

With its towering volcano, lush rainforests and beautiful beaches, St. Kitts offers a full menu of hikes, ranging from soothing walks along powdery beaches to rigorous climbs on mountain trails. Guided tours of the rainforest are popular; a far more strenuous hike is up to the crater rim of Mt. Liamuiga, an all-day, challenging excursion.

Don't miss the **petroglyphs**, located near Romney Manor, carved many years ago by the Carib Indians. While you're stopped here, check out the handicrafts sold next door by a neighbor who creates turtles and bird feeders from coconut shells.

Just beyond the petroglyphs lies **Caribelle Batik**, Romney Manor, *Tel. 869/465-6253*, a stop worth making even if you don't want to shop. Here you can watch batik in progress and buy the finished product in the form of shirts, wraps, and wall hangings. (Even if you don't want to buy, it's worth a trip to Romney Manor just to visit the ruins of the stately greathouse and the grounds shaded by trees that date back hundreds of years.) The closest thing that St. Kitts has to a botanical garden, these grounds are home to many tropical plant species. You can't miss the huge **Saman tree**, said to be the largest tree in the Caribbean. On the drive to Caribelle Batik, look for the historic aqueducts along the side of the road, a reminder of the island's early water system.

Rainforest and volcano tours are available from several operators. **Greg's Safaris**, Basseterre, St. Kitts, West Indies, *Tel. 869/465-4121*, offers a half-day guided Rainforest Safari through mountain trails into the Oceanic Rainforest. Visitors have a chance to look for birdlife, cross springs, identify exotic wildflowers, and enjoy the mist shrouded forest.

SIGHTS

Greg's Safari's also offers a full-day **Mt. Liamuiga Volcano Hike**. This strenuous trip includes a rugged hike up the volcano to view the mile-wide crater rim, and a chance to see the cloud forest and steaming sulphur vents in the volcanic region. The hike is a tough one, so come prepared with very good walking shoes.

Nevis

It's a short flight or a relaxing catamaran ride from St. Kitts to nearby Nevis, home to two spectacular beaches. **Pinney's Beach** is one of the island's best; the waters here are protected by reefs and are popular with snorkelers, swimmers and sunbathers. **Oualie** (pronounced Wally) **Beach** is the most active beach on Nevis, with watersport operations and a splendid view of St. Kitts. Nature lovers can also visit the **Botanical Gardens of Nevis**, *www.botanicalgardennevis.com*, located on the grounds of the original Montpelier plantation. Today the garden is an excellent introduction to the many flowers and trees which dot this island paradise.

The main community on Nevis is the city of **Charlestown**. Any day except Sunday, the place to be in Charlestown is the outdoor Market Place, bustling with vendors offering Caribbean fruits, vegetables and seafood.

Caribbean history buffs will find two interesting museums on Nevis. In Charlestown, the **Museum of Nevis History** includes exhibits on the indigenous residents of Nevis who called the island home approximately 4,000 years ago, as well as the island's political history, slavery, home crafts, churches and more. The museum is located in the house that was the birthplace of Alexander Hamilton, first Secretary of the US Treasury. Another excellent stop is the **Nelson Museum**, containing the largest collection of Horatio Nelson memorabilia in the Western hemisphere. Paintings, china, figurines, and remembrances of the naval leader are found here, along with displays on Nevisian history.

SHOPPING

Ready for a little ghost story? Time to make a stop at the **Eden Brown Estate**. These ruins, formerly an estate of a wealthy planter, were the site of a true tragedy. The legend goes that on the eve of his wedding, a bridegroom planter and his best man got into a duel and both men were killed. The bride-to-be went mad and is said to haunt the ruins today. The site is grown over and is little more than a few stone walls, but for those with an active imagination it's an interesting stop.

BEST SHOPPING

The best shopping stop is St. Kitts' **Caribelle Batik** at Romney Manor. Here you can watch **batik** in progress and hear an explanation of the step-by-step process involved. You can buy the finished product in the form of shirts, wraps, and wall hangings. Prices are reasonable and the batik makes a colorful souvenir of your island visit. We purchased a batik of a string band that brings back good memories of our island stays.

Even if you don't want to buy, it's worth a trip to Romney Manor just to visit the stately greathouse and the grounds shaded by trees that date back hundreds of years. The grounds here are some of the most beautiful in the Leeward Islands.

In Basseterre, duty-free devotees will find plenty of selection at **Pelican Mall** on the waterfront. This two-story mall, designed with Kittitian architecture and tropical colors, features duty-free shops selling everything from china to liquor to Cuban cigars. Twenty-six shops make this a popular stop, especially for cruise ship passengers who come in from the new cruise ship berth adjacent.

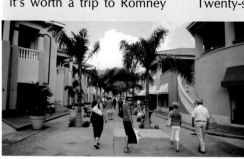

Stamp collectors will be familiar with

Nevis because of its often-sought stamps. Stop by the Philatelic Bureau in Charlestown for the best selection. While you're in Charlestown, stop by the **Handicraft Cooperative**. Located near the Bureau of Tourism, this little shop is a must for arts and crafts shoppers and anyone looking to bring back a Nevisian souvenir. Look for wood carvings, small artwork, and even Nevisian honey here.

One of the best stops is **Nevis Pottery** in Newcastle, where artisans craft the local clay soil into various vessels. The pots are finished over a fire of coconut shells behind the shop. The shop is open Monday through Friday and is located near the Newcastle Airport.

BEST SLEEPS & EATS

ST. KITTS
Ottley's Plantation Inn $$$-$$$$
Legend has it that this 18th-century greathouse is haunted, but that doesn't stop the vacationers who come here looking for peace and quiet. Guest rooms in the greathouse and in nearby cottages are nestled on 35-acres of tropical grounds. Along with golf and tennis, guests can explore a small rain forest on the grounds and search for vervet monkeys. Visitors have access to a nearby black sand beach. *Info: Tel. 800/772-3039 or 869/465-7234, www.ottleys.com.*

Rawlins Plantation $$$
As far back as 1690 a plantation now named Rawlins began producing sugar. Nearly 300 years later, the greathouse, burned in an early fire, was reconstructed and opened as an inn. Today the chief activity around here is pure relaxation. The most romantic of the hideaway's 12 rooms is the honeymoon suite,

SLEEPS & EATS

housed in a 300-year old sugar mill. Guests climb a winding stair from the downstairs living room to the upstairs bedroom perch, its walls made of volcanic stone. *Info: Tel. 869/465-6221, www.rawlinsplantation.com.*

St. Kitts Marriott Resort & Royal Beach Casino $$-$$$
The St. Kitts Marriott Resort and The Royal Beach Casino, with over 500 rooms, offers a full menu of activities ranging from golf to sailing, diving to rainforest walks. The resort includes three pools as well as a kids' club. When it's time to step out of the sun, try a game of Texas Hold'em or three card poker at the 35,000-square-foot Royal Beach Casino or indulge in a little pampering in one of the eight treatment rooms at the Emerald Mist Spa before enjoying a romantic repast at one of the resort's eight restaurants, which offer menus featuring both international and Caribbean cuisine. *Info: Tel. 869/466-1200 or 800/236-2427, www.marriott.com.*

A TYPICAL MEAL
A meal in St. Kitts and Nevis means traditional Caribbean fare such as snapper, grouper, salt fish or even flying fish accompanied by side dishes such as breadfruit, pumpkin, yams, and the obligatory rice and (pigeon) peas. Everything will be flavorful and often spicy. Wash down dinner with the local beer, Carib.

Fisherman's Wharf $$
Relax in the informal seaside atmosphere at this open-air dinner restaurant featuring local dishes. The restaurant itself is located on a wharf and offers romantic views of Basseterre at night. *Info: Ocean Terrace Inn, Fortlands, Basseterre, Tel. 869/ 465-2754.*

Rawlins Plantation $$
Guests and non-guests stop by Rawlins Plantation for the daily West Indian lunch buffet. The buffet features local favorites such as saffron rice, curried chicken, and flying fish fritters, followed by soursop sorbet. The dishes are prepared using fresh seafood and herbs and vegetables. *Info: Rawlins Plantation Inn, Mount Pleasant, Tel. 869/465-6221, www.rawlinsplantation.com.*

Royal Palm $$$
Often cited as one of the island's top restaurants, the prix fixe menu features dishes such as Kittitan Tomato Dill Bisque, pan seared red snapper, and roast herb infused tenderloin of prime beef. *Info: Ottley's Plantation Inn, Tel. 869/465-7234, www.ottleys.com/royal.php.*

NEVIS

Four Seasons Resort Nevis $$$$
Damaged by Hurricane Omar in 2008, plans call to reopen this elegant resort in November 2009. The 196-room resort at Pinney's Beach is the most luxurious accommodation on Nevis and indeed one of the top resorts in the Caribbean. Boasting a championship golf course, 10 tennis  courts, two outdoor Jacuzzis, 24-hour room service, and more, this resort is for those looking for a little pampering. The Four Seasons Nevis sprawls across grounds dotted with coconut palms and other carefully tended fauna. Guests can enjoy a round of golf, scuba, windsurf, or just sun around the pool, cooled by Evian sprayed on guests by mindful pool attendants. *Info: Tel. 869/469-1111, 800/819-5053 US and Canada, www.fourseasons.com.*

Golden Rock Inn $$
Eco-tourists are attracted to Golden Rock because of the diligent efforts of its owner, Pam Barry. A fifth-generation Nevisian, Barry emphasizes local culture, history, and nature studies, offering her self-guided nature trails to both guests and non-guests alike. The most romantic room at this historic plantation inn is the two-story sugar windmill. *Info: Tel. 869/469-3346, www.golden-rock.com.*

Hermitage Plantation Inn $$$
When magazines look for a classically Caribbean setting for

fashion shoots, they've often selected the mountainside Hermit-age Inn, housed in a greathouse constructed around 1700. Sprinkled around grounds bursting with tropical blooms, are restored plantation cottages that serve as guest rooms for those looking for the ultimate in privacy. Guests have access to a swimming pool and tennis courts as well as romantic pursuits such as carriage rides and horseback riding. *Info: Tel. 800/682-4025 or 869/469-3477, www.hermitagenevis.com.*

Montpelier Plantation Inn $$$$

This historic Nevis inn transports guests to an age of elegance with leisurely fine dining, quiet gardens, and vacations uninter-rupted by telephones. The setting for this time transport starts with the grounds of the inn. On March 11, 1787, Admiral Horatio Nelson married Fanny Nisbet in front of a royal audience on the lawn of Montpelier Plantation. Like many couples that choose a Caribbean wedding, Nelson and Nisbet exchanged their vows outdoors, in the shade of a massive silk cotton tree. Prince William Henry, who eventually would become King William IV of Great Britain, gave away the bride, a well-known Nevisian widow, to the officer whose naval career was legendary.

Although much of the original plantation later fell into disrepair, the silk cotton tree remains a testament to the regal wedding. Today the stately tree still greets visitors at this elegantly reno-vated 17-room hotel, a place where brushes with royalty did not end with the Nelson wedding. The late Princess Diana and her sons once opted for Montpelier's quiet seclusion on the lower slopes of Mount Nevis. Whether seeking a break from the limelight or just a few days of peace and quiet, most guests appreciate the hotel's somewhat dignified British air.

Activities include tennis, swimming (there is a freshwater pool and a shuttle to the hotel's private beach) and hikes led by local ecologists for a look at the island's rainforest and former sugar plantations. Golf can be arranged at the Four Season's Robert Trent Jones II championship course. Activity buffs can also enjoy windsurfing, horseback riding, water skiing, scuba diving, deep sea fishing and sailing — all arranged by the hotel. And for nature lovers, just a five-minute walk from the inn stands the Botanical Garden of Nevis, located on the grounds of the original plantation. Today the garden is an excellent introduction to the many flowers and trees which dot this island paradise.

For pure relaxation, guests schedule a visit to The Spa at Four Seasons Resort Nevis, with treatments ranging from a mango sea salt glow to the "rum tonic," a cocktail of a treatment which begins with a sugar cane exfoliation before a slathering of rum, ginger and honey glaze.

The 16 guest rooms and one suite at the resort echo the mellow style of the property, a tropical decor interpreted with contemporary touches including pencil post beds and rich fabrics. Off each room a private verandah invites travelers to savor the tropical tranquility for which this island is known. All guests receive a full breakfast and afternoon tea, complete with fresh scones.

Guest rooms have large tile bathrooms with a shower and tub, overhead fans, in-room safes, and elegant touches such as Gilchrist & Soames amenities. All rooms are cooled by tropical breezes as well as air-conditioning. To preserve the peace and quiet, no rooms have telephones. *Info: Tel. 869/469-3462, www.montpeliernevis.com.*

Nisbet Plantation Beach Club $$$$

This plantation was the former home of Admiral Nelson's bride, Fanny Nisbet. The plantation today is a 36-room inn boasting one of Nevis's most striking vistas: a quarter-mile palm-lined walk from the greathouse to one of Nevis's finest beaches. Guests stay in lemon-tinted bungalows scattered throughout the property. Today the greathouse of this former coconut plantation is home

SLEEPS & EATS

to an elegant restaurant and bar. Other facilities include beach, pool, and tennis courts. *Info: Tel. 869/469-9325 or 800/742-6008, www.nisbetplantation.com.*

Coconuts $$

Coconuts offers a full breakfast, which might include dishes such as Eggs Benedict Florentine, Nevisian saltfish with coconut johnny cake, or Caribbean Toast. And for those couples who can't tear themselves away from the romance of their little hideaway cottage, continental breakfast can also be served in your room. *Info: Tel. 869/469-9325, 800/742-6008, www.nisbetplantation.com.*

The Dining Room $$$

Although for lunch many Four Seasons guests head to the resort's

grill, for an elegant dinner they move to the great house's dining room. This elegant eatery offers diners a candlelight meal and serves many local seafood specialties accompanied by an extensive wine list. *Info: Four Seasons Nevis, Tel. 869/469-1111.*

Great House Restaurant $$$

At Nisbet's Great House, which dates back to the earliest days of the sugar plantation that began in 1778, dinner is a highlight of the day. This two-story great house, with a wide, screened veranda across the back, is today home to a fine restaurant. Start your evening with a drink at the Great House bar then step out on the verandah for a memorable meal accompanied by fine wine. *Info: Tel. 869/469-9325 or 800/742-6008, www.nisbetplantation.com.*

PRACTICAL MATTERS

Currency. The Eastern Caribbean (EC) dollar is legal tender. It is exchanged at a rate fixed to the US dollar: $1 US = 2.7 EC.

Driving. Driving is British style on both islands, on the LEFT side of the road.

Getting There. Most visitors first arrive at St. Kitts' Robert Llewelyn Bradshaw International Airport (formerly Golden Rock Airport) with jet service from the US. Service into Nevis is available on American Eagle via San Juan, Puerto Rico. Ferry companies also provide daily service between St. Kitts and Nevis; for a schedule of the 45-minute trips, visit *www.nevisisland.com/SeaTransportation.htm*.

Information. St. Kitts Tourism Authority, *Tel. 800/582-6208 (US) or 888-395-4887 (Canada)*; Nevis Tourism Authority, *Tel. 866/ 55-NEVIS* (US and Canada) or *869/469-7550. www.stkittstourism.kn* and *www.nevisisland.com*.

13. ST. LUCIA

We first heard **St. Lucia** before we saw it. Flying in from the States near the midnight hour, we stepped off the prop plane and instantly received a warm welcome from the humid night winds. Just yards away, we could hear the sound of the Caribbean lapping against the shoreline, right off the Vigie Airport runway.

But the next morning we learned what St. Lucia was really about. Jagged peaks clothed in velvety tropical plants. Honey-colored beaches shaded by towering palms. And everywhere, everywhere, colorful blooms and greenery that promised romantic walks in a true garden of Eden.

INTRO

St. Lucia is a tropical wonderland, a place where every hill, valley, and roadside is a veritable garden. Orange, lime, lemon, mango (over 100 varieties, we learned), breadfruit, plum, and coffee trees cover the landscape. Pineapples sprout alongside the highway. Spices like vanilla, nutmeg, and cinnamon grow in thick profusion.

But most evident are the **bananas**. Not just banana trees, but banana plantations. Miles of bananas that stretch to the horizon. Along with its reputation as a drive-through grocery market, St. Lucia is also abloom with color. Tall flame flowers. Orchids. Hibiscus. Shrimp plants. Like an explosion of a thousand florist shops.

The island's most famous landmarks are the **Pitons**, two mountain peaks located in the southwest region of the island. The 2,620-foot **Gros Piton** and the 2,460-foot **Petit Piton** rear abruptly from the sea's edge; these volcanic peaks are reserved for experienced climbers who dare to snake their way up the misty, jungle-covered, boulder-strewn mountainsides. The reward for the half-day trek up Gros Piton or the longer slog up the steeper Petit Piton? Huge views well worth the trouble.

With such spectacular scenery, it's easy to see why St. Lucia is nicknamed the "Helen of the West Indies," St. Lucia is one of the most beautiful islands in the Caribbean. The 238-square mile landform is rich with jagged mountains, lush valleys, rugged cliffs, and pristine beaches that come in various shades of black and beige.

The pear-shaped island becomes increasingly lush and mountainous the further south you travel. The capital city of **Castries**, lo-

144 OPEN ROAD'S BEST OF THE CARIBBEAN

cated on the northwest shore, is home to much of the island's industry. Further south, the island's agricultural district offers miles of banana plantations. On the southwest coast, the community of **Soufriere** stands just miles from the dense rain forest and in view of St. Lucia's two landmarks: Gros Piton and Petit Piton. These two peaks have been scaled by experienced climbers, who rate the ascent as difficult.

Unlike most Caribbean islands, St. Lucia is served by two international airports, so pay close attention here. More than one traveler has booked flights into one airport only to discover that their hotel was across the island, over an hour's (expensive) taxi ride away.

The main airport is Hewanorra, located on the southern end of the island. On the northern end of the island lies George F. L. Charles Airport (formerly named—and still locally called—Vigie Airport) in the city of Castries. This airport is closest to the bulk of the island's hotel properties, but it is served primarily by smaller carriers.

For years, St. Lucia was notorious for its poor roads, winding potholed terrors that made travel slow and uncomfortable. In 1995, however, the island completed a major road refurbishment project, and we're glad to say that we found travel from one end of the island to the other both speedy and easy.

Taxis are the most common means of transportation for vacationers, but be advised that a journey from the north end of the island to the Piton region is expensive. Rental cars are available from the airports and the major hotels. You'll need to obtain a local license from the immigration desk at either airport, police station, or from the larger rental dealers. You will also need to present your local driver's license.

Taxis can also be rented by the hour for a private tour. Work out the price with the driver before you leave. Tour companies also offer a wide array of guided full- and half-day tours of the island. Visit the rain forest in open-air jeep (book early for this one since space is limited), take a bus tour to the volcano, the botanical gardens, and the waterfalls, or enjoy a combination tour with a drive down the coast and a catamaran ride back.

🚶 BEST SIGHTS IN ST. LUCIA

SIGHTS

On the northern reach of the island lies **Pigeon Island**, a 35-minute drive from Castries. No longer a true island but connected to the main island by causeway, Pigeon Island has a long history as everything from a pirate hideout to a military fort. The ruins of the fort can still be seen at Pigeon Island National Park, a popular day trip for north shore vacationers and the site of many of St. Lucia's festivals.

Most guests stay on the northeast section of St. Lucia near **Castries**, the island's largest city with a population of 60,000. This capital city was destroyed by fire several times, but some colonial period wooden structures still remain. You'll see several of them as you head south on Government House Road. This twisting, climbing slice of road is slow going but offers you a great view. Save time for a stop across from the Governor's House for a panoramic look at the city. From atop **Morne Fortune**, hill of good luck (not such good luck for the French soldiers who resided here in the 18th century; they were plagued by yellow fever), you'll have a postcard view over Castries Harbour, Vigie Peninsula and Pigeon Island.

Continuing south, the road soon drops into a veritable forest: the first of several **banana plantations**. Driving past this display of the island's number one crop, you'll see blue plastic bags hanging from many trees. These cover the bananas themselves to shield the crop from insects and bruising by the banana leaves. The banana plant yields only one crop during its lifetime, a process that takes nine months to bear fruit.

Marigot Harbour, located just off the main road, is the next stop. This magical harbor, often considered to be the most beautiful in the Caribbean, is dotted with yachts from around the globe. If you don't have your own, don't worry.

SIGHTS

The Moorings, a company headquartered in the British Virgin Islands, can rent you a yacht with or without a crew to enjoy a sailing vacation of your own. Landlubbers will enjoy the scenic harbor as well, and may recognize it from the movie *Dr. Doolittle*.

South of Marigot, the road passes through many small communities and fishing villages. Make time for a walk around **Anse La Raye** (Beach of the Ray), a traditional St. Lucian fishing village. Stroll along the waterfront to view the hand-crafted fishing canoes painted in bright primary colors and the various fishing nets and traps used in these waters. In town, you'll see traditional Caribbean homes with lawns outlined in conch shells, the large Roman Catholic church, and an authentic Creole bakery.

The **Soufriere** region is the heartland of the island's many attractions. There's no denying that the most scenic part of the island is this south-central region. Starting with the rain forest and continuing down to the Pitons, this spectacular area is the breadbasket of the island. Every tropi-

cal fruit and vegetable thrives in this rich region, which is sparsely populated.

For many travelers, the most fascinating area is the **rain forest**. You'll need a guide to enter the restricted rain forest region, so sign up for a guided tour with one of the island's tour operators. Hiking tours are available with guides from the Forestry Department. You'll walk through the dense foliage, **swim in a tropical waterfall**, and learn more about the plants that make up this fragile ecosystem. And, if you're lucky, you may have the opportunity to see the rare St. Lucian parrot.

This area is also home to the unique **Sulphur Spring volcano**, often nicknamed the "drive-through volcano." Although visitors can no longer walk among the bubbling pools for safety reasons, you'll find viewing stations along the edge of the caldera, perfect for snapping a photo of the steaming cauldrons. The smell of sulphur hangs heavy in the air, thanks to water black with ash that percolates with gases released from deep in the earth's core. (Leave your silver jewelry back at the ho-

SIGHTS

tel for this trip. The gases can cause silver to tarnish.)

Near the volcano, the **Diamond Waterfalls and Gardens** bloom with tropical splendor. A flower-lined trail winds to Diamond Waterfalls, a cascade that leaves a spray of "diamond" twinkles suspended in the air. Most days, you can slip into steamy mineral baths built among ruins of the first baths commissioned by French King Louis XVI for use by his troops in the late 1700s.

BEST FESTIVAL

St. Lucia 's biggest event takes place for one week in May. The **St. Lucia Jazz Festival** draws international superstars for outdoor performances at Pigeon Island as well as other venues including Soufriere, Castries' Derek Walcott Square, Pointe Seraphine, beach venues, and more. In the past, top names such as Beres Hammond, Patti Labelle, and Chaka Khan have drawn international crowds to this popular festival. *Info: stluciajazz.org.*

BEST SHOPPING

SHOPPING

Castries, the island's largest town, is also its top shopping area. There are malls and markets for everything from fine jewels to handmade crafts that capture the island spirit.

Pointe Seraphine is the island's duty-free port. You'll find well-known chains such as Little Switzerland, Colom-

bian Emeralds and Benetton. (Remember to bring your passport and return airline tickets to take advantage of the duty-free shopping. Items can be taken with you at point of purchase.) Pointe Seraphine is open weekdays, and on Saturdays, until 1 pm only. Like most shops in St. Lucia, the mall is closed on Sundays.

Outside of Castries, make a stop at **Caribelle Batik** for handmade batik shirts, wraps, and scarves. In **Choiseul**, stop by the **Choiseul Arts and Crafts Center**. This town is known as the crafts center of the island, and here you'll find straw, wood, and clay handcrafts, all manufactured locally.

BEST SPORTS & RECREATION

Another major attraction of St. Lucia is its **scuba diving**. Anse Chastanet is considered to be the top dive spot on the island and one of the best in the Caribbean. The reason? Extraordinary fish life, coral formations, and sponge growth right off shore. Divers and snorkelers can enjoy spectacular underwater exploration just yards from the beach.

St. Lucia's **beaches** run from golden brown to a salt-and-pepper mixture of sand and volcanic elements. Some of the most popular beaches are Anse Chastanet, Anse Cochon, and Reduit Beach. Sunbathers take note: topless and nude sunbathing is prohibited throughout St. Lucia.

As the sun sinks into the sea, don't think that the fun is over in St. Lucia, especially on Friday nights. **Gros Islet**, a small island off the north shore, is known throughout the Caribbean for its Friday night jump-up. Street side music blares and visitors and locals alike jam to the sounds of reggae, soca, and calypso—a true Caribbean celebration.

BEST SLEEPS & EATS

Anse Chastanet $$$$
For vacationers looking to put as little as possible between the Caribbean and themselves, St. Lucia's Anse Chastanet offers a place where the barriers between guests and the great outdoors are frequently as minimal as three exterior walls.

The vision of architect Nick Troubetzkoy, this hillside resort rises from a palm-lined bay to offer views of St. Lucia's spectacular twin Piton mountains. The architect-owner designed this singular resort to scale the hillside with guest accommodations that offer visitors open-air showers, trees that sprout right up through guest rooms, and open walls where views are uninterrupted by windows or screens.

The resort atmosphere is pure St. Lucian. The resort utilizes island-made furnishings, cloths, foods, and artwork both to offer the guests a genuine island experience and to nurture the culture and economy of St. Lucia. The simple guest rooms are decorated in West Indian style, with furniture that is produced on St. Lucia, usually from the Soufriere region. Beds, chairs, and couches are covered in a simple cotton madras, the national cloth of St. Lucia. Amenities include hair dryers, refrigerators, coffee makers, and ceiling fans. Although they're not always necessary, for guests' convenience mosquito nets are provided, along with electric mosquito coils. Telephones are not available in rooms; an outdoor bank of phones for guest use is located near the main office. Guests check for messages on a chalkboard posted nearby. *Info: Tel. 758/459-7000 or 800/223-1108, www.ansechastanet.com.*

SLEEPS & EATS

Coco Palm $-$$

Looking for a hip boutique hotel that won't hurt your budget? St. Lucia's new Coco Palm Hotel just might be the answer. Located  in the center of Rodney Bay Village, Coco Palm has 71 rooms and 12 suites. Among the resort's best features are the signature swim-up rooms that allow guests to literally step into Coco Palm's free form swimming pool from their terrace. Coco Palm's grand suites offer two full bathrooms, a living room (with a pull-out sofa bed) and a terrace. All rooms feature modern amenities such as air conditioning, DVD players, Wi-Fi, Direct TV, CD players, cordless phones and bathrooms with glass-walled shower stalls and "rain shower" heads. Coco Palm is located in the heart of Rodney Bay Village, the island's hot spot for cuisine and nightly entertainment. Rodney Bay Village is the place for any traveler to feel like a native St. Lucian as tourists and locals drink, dance, and dine together. The hotel is a two-minute walk through Rodney Bay Village to Reduit Beach, voted the best beach on the island. *Info: Tel. 866/588-5980 or 758/456-2800, www.coco-resorts.com.*

Coconut Bay Beach Resort & Spa $$-$$$

Constructed with two separate wings, this all-inclusive St. Lucia sanctuary located near Vieux Fort allows the dreams of a perfect vacation to take flight for both adults and kids. While couples de-stress at the Kai Mer Spa or at the 18 and over only pool at the Adult Oasis section of the 254- guest room resort, families can feel free to frolic about at the Family Playground wing. Everyone at the 254-guest room retreat can enjoy the pools, basketball and tennis courts. *Info: Tel. 758/459-6000 or 877/352-8898, www.cbayresort.com.*

SLEEPS & EATS

Jade Mountain $$$$

If you like Anse Chastanet (above), you'll love Jade Mountain. Perched above its sister property and also a creation of architect Nick Troubetzkoy, Jade Mountain opened in Fall 2006. With 24 three-walled suites with private infinity pools, the property operates as a resort within a resort at Anse Chastanet. Like Anse Chastanet, rooms are technology free with no phones or internet connections. The exclusive resort features a boutique spa, a restaurant showcasing James Beard award winner Chef Allen Susser, and more. *Info: Tel. 800/223-1108 or 758/459-4000, www.jademountain.com.*

Ladera Resort $$$$

Tucked between the Pitons, this intimate hillside resort features villas and suites, many with private pools. This unique property

offers six villa suites and 25 suites, each a three-walled unit that's open on one side to reveal the mountain views. All accommodations include a pool or a plunge pool enjoyed in complete privacy. *Info: Tel. 866/290-0978 or 758/459-6618, www.ladera.com.*

Sandals Grande St. Lucian Spa & Beach Resort $$$-$$$$

Like other Sandals resorts, this resort is a veritable honeycomb of activity from the bars and billiards room in its elegant lobby to the tennis, golf, and watersports offerings. Of course, if you and your partner want to be alone, that's all right, too. You can hang out by the freeform pools, daysail in a Sunfish, or dine by candlelight. Unlike other Sandals resorts, however, this resort is home to the exclusive Millionaire's Suites, named because each cost a million dollars to construct and offers views to match. The resort also offers swim-up rooms, rondoval rooms, and butler service in some categories. *Info: Tel. 888/SANDALS, www.sandals.com.*

SLEEPS & EATS

Auberge Seraphine $$-$$$

This seafood restaurant, with a sprinkling of French and Caribbean dishes, serves both lunch and dinner. Start with grilled calamari or Gros Islet-style fish cakes served with tamarind sauce, then try the breadfruit vichyssoise or Caribbean fish chowder. Entrees range from curried shrimp with coconuts to Caribbean lobster to St. Lucian style chicken, stuffed with green bananas and served on a bed of callaloo. Reservations are suggested. *Info: Vigie Yacht Marina, Castries, Tel. 758/453-2073.*

Bang $-$$

What a location! Tucked between the magnificent mountains, this waterfront restaurant specializes in jerk barbecue. Reservations are suggested. *Info: Soufriere, Tel. 758/459-7864.*

Dasheene $$-$$$

Open for breakfast, lunch and dinner, this casually elegant restaurant offers spectacular mountain views. Look for specialties including the award-winning pan fried Shrimp Dasheene, Dasheene Lucian Lamb Curry, rasta pasta, and fisherman's catch but save room for the Ladera Coco Orlando's Chocolate Rum Mousse served with a coconut waffle. *Info: Ladera Resort, Tel. 866/290-0978, www.ladera.com.*

The Great House $$$

On Friday nights, save time before Gros Islet's famous jump-up for dinner at this elegant plantation-style restaurant, located at Cap Estate. Enjoy a candlelight dinner of lime grilled dorado, rack of lamb with mint sauce, jerk pork, or a local favorite, curried chicken and mango with rice. Finish off with truly sinful desserts: coconut cheesecake with tropical fruit toppings, passion fruit mousse, or soursop ice cream in filo pastry. *Info: Gros Islet, Tel. 758/450-0450.*

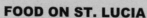

FOOD ON ST. LUCIA

Creole food is the order of the day in restaurants across St. Lucia. Spices liven up beef, chicken, pork, and lamb dishes, all served up with favorites such as rice and peas, dasheen (a root vegetable similar to a potato), and plantains. Enjoy it with a taste of local spirits such as La Belle Creole, Bounty Rum, and Piton beer.

The Still $

This is one of our favorite St. Lucian diners, a delightful local eatery that dishes out tasty local cuisine, much of it utilizing produce grown right on property. Family-owned, the service is friendly and if you see something that you don't recognize, just ask. We dined on Creole chicken served with mango salad, rice, beans, and yam pie. Don't expect anything fancy here, but this is the place to come for lunch or dinner for a true taste of Creole cooking at a very reasonable price. *Info: Soufriere, Tel. 758/459-7224.*

The Treehouse $$$

Like its name suggests, this restaurant sits perched, tree level, on a steep hillside. Fortunately, the view is matched by the food here. We started with coconut crusted local crab backs, then moved on to a creamy celery and bacon soup. Entrees include pork medallions with a light mustard sauce, vegetarian roti on curried lentils, grilled dorado, St. Lucian beef pepperpot, and other dishes using local products. The wine list here is excellent as well. Breakfast is served daily and dinner is served daily except Tuesday. *Info: Anse Chastanet, Soufriere, Tel. 800/223-1108.*

PRACTICAL MATTERS

Currency. The Eastern Caribbean (EC) dollar is the official currency. The exchange rate is fixed to the US dollar at US $1 equals EC $2.70.

Electricity. 220 volts, 50 cycles. Some hotels offer 110 volts, 60 cycles. Also, socket styles vary, although most are the three-pin style with square plugs (UK).

Getting There. Unlike most Caribbean islands, St. Lucia is served by two international airports, so pay close attention here. More than one traveler has booked flights into one airport only to discover that their hotel was across the island, over an hour's (expensive) taxi ride away.

The main airport is **Hewanorra**, located on the southern end of the island. It's the larger of the two airports, with jet service from major carriers. Hotels near the Pitons are only a short taxi ride from the Hewanorra terminal.

On the northern end of the island lies **George F. L. Charles Airport** (formerly Vigie Airport although many still call it by that name), located in the city of Castries. This is closest to the bulk of the island's hotel properties, but it is served by smaller carriers offering primarily service within the Caribbean.

Information. St. Lucia Tourist Board, *Tel. 800/4-ST-LUCIA*

Website. *www.stlucia.org*

14. ST. MARTIN/SINT MAARTEN

Fine French food. Topless French beaches. Dutch architecture. Casinos that ring with baccarat and roulette.

This is **St. Martin**, the island that calls itself "a little bit European and a lot Caribbean." Located 150 miles southeast of Puerto Rico, this 37-square-mile island is occupied by **Dutch Sint Maarten** and **French St. Martin**, the smallest land mass on the globe shared by two nations.

Today you'll find that the line between the French and Dutch sides is the simplest border crossing you'll ever make. No passports. No customs. No immigration. Just a simple sign marking the demarcation between two nations.

INTRO

The island's Dutch influence goes back to 1631 when the Dutch decided to take a role in West Indian trade. Spain and Holland fought over the island for several years, and in the meantime, France slid into the picture. Finally, the Dutch and the French were left to work things out and to split the island between the powers.

No one knows exactly how the triangular island was divided, but the popular legend is that a Frenchman and a Dutchman walked in opposite directions around the perimeter of the island with the understanding that the points where they met would become the new border. One tale says the Frenchman took water and the Dutchman beer, causing him to get sleepy and cover less ground. The R-rated version of the fable claims that the Frenchman enticed a young maid to divert the Dutchman for a few hours, helping the Frenchman claim 21 square miles to the Dutchman's 16.

C'est la vie.

Although the border is almost superficial, there are distinctions between the two countries. Mention "St. Martin" and many visitors will immediately think of topless bathing that's de rigeur on the Gallic beaches. And on one mile and a half stretch, au natural is the order of the day. Orient Beach or Baie Orientale is the home of Club Orient, a naturist resort. The public beach is an equal mixture of nudists and cruise ship gawkers, sprinkled with folks who just want to enjoy gentle surf and powdery sand the color of toasted coconut.

Most visitors arrive in Simpson Bay's Princess Juliana International Airport. This is one of the Caribbean's busiest airports, with direct service from New York, Newark, Miami, Baltimore, and San Juan — not to mention Paris and Amsterdam. Regional air service to many small islands also travels through this hub.

On the northwestern side of St. Martin you'll find the culinary capital of **Grand Case**. Home to restaurants that perch at the pinnacle of Caribbean dining, both in taste and price, Grand Case also offers a true island dining experience at the Loos (pronounced lows). Wander among this stretch of outdoor stalls and order barbecue or lobster, freshly grilled and often highly seasoned.

South of Grand Case lies

Marigot, home of the market. Here you can shop with locals for spices from throughout the Caribbean, as well as souvenirs such as batik clothing, wood carvings, and Haitian art, produced by the many Haitian refugees who relocated to this French island.

Continue south and soon you'll reach the Dutch border and **Simpson Bay**. This is the most urbanized area of the island, dotted with high rise hotels and condominiums, chic boutiques, and pulsating nightspots. Simpson Bay hops with vacationers who come to enjoy pristine beaches, the island's best snorkeling at **Mullet Bay**, and the only golf course on the island, but in nearby **Philipsburg** it's shopping that draws visitors.

Duty-free shops line the busy streets, and pedestrians can spend an entire day popping from store to store in this commercial center. Cameras, electronic goods, perfumes, and fine jewelry are especially good buys.

The Dutch influence is felt far less strongly in Sint Maarten than the Gallic influence in St. Martin. Although the official language taught in the schools, Dutch is rarely heard on the street. And although it falls under the government of the Netherlands Antilles and the Kingdom of the Netherlands, the US dollar reigns here. The atmosphere is strictly West Indian with an eye toward American commerce. US dollars are accepted freely and shopping on the Dutch side is more American-style than in St. Martin, which features more European-style shops with pricing in Euros. (In today's tough economic climate and less favorable US exchange rate, the Dutch side of the island has seen a boom in business because pricing is in US dollars.)

Taxis are one of the best ways to get around the island, especially for the first time visitor. Steep, winding roads combined with plentiful traffic can be challenging the first day or two, so consider a taxi for the first part of your stay. Taxis travel freely to both sides of the island.

If you'll be traveling extensively during your stay, however, a rental car can be a good invest-

ment. Taxi rates from end to end of the island quickly surpass rental rates. You'll find that most rental companies offer free pickup and delivery service. To rent a vehicle, you'll need a valid driver's license and a major credit card. Driving throughout the island is on the RIGHT side of the road.

Public buses are available and offer an inexpensive and colorful (although not the fastest) way to travel the island. Buses run from Marigot to Philipsburg, other routes travel to Mullet Bay, Simpson Bay, Cole Bay, and Grand Case. Buses run from about 6am to midnight and can be flagged down anywhere. They leave every hour from Grand Case.

When a cruise ship is in port in Philipsburg, you can often find cheap transportation to Orient Beach. Look for taxi drivers holding an Orient Beach sign; vans shuttle back and forth for just a few dollars per person.

Traffic in Philipsburg can be unreal, though; plan your trips to avoid peak commuting times as well as times when the drawbridge opens and traffic backs up for what seems like miles.

BEST SIGHTS IN ST. MARTIN/SINT MAARTEN 🚶

SIGHTS

Looking for something to do on land? St. Martin has 40 kilometers of trails of varying difficulties. The most cited hike is the walk between Paradise Peak (**Pic Paradis**), at 1,391 feet the highest point on the island, and Concordia. From these heights, hikers enjoy a look at the island from observation decks. Less strenuous but offering a good view is the walk up the stairs to the restored **Fort St. Louis** for a panoramic view of Marigot.

Another top sightseeing stop is the **Butterfly Farm**, *www.thebutterflyfarm.com*, located on the French side of

the island near Orient Bay. You'll walk among free-flying butterflies in this fascinating display.

Most travelers spend at least part of a day in **Philipsburg**, the largest community on the island and the capital of the Dutch side. The most distinctive structure in town is the **Courthouse**, a green and white building constructed in 1793 and renovated just a few years ago. It's a popular meeting site for shoppers on Frontstreet and the taxi stand is located nearby. On Frontstreet, the **St. Maarten Museum** is housed in a restored 19th century West In-

BEST FESTIVAL

For over four decades, **Sint Maarten** has hosted a popular carnival usually planned for late April. The fun includes the traditional **Carnival** fun of Jouvert, a massive jump up that begins at 3am and works its way around Great Salt Pond. A large Carnival parade, calypso competitions, numerous concerts, carnival royalty and more fill the carnival days and nights. It's all topped off by Closing Jump Up or Last Lap when Carnival Band of the Year is named. The event culminates with the march of King MoMo; symbolizing the sins of the year, King MoMo is burned in effigy at the end of the parade. For more information and next year's dates, visit *www.stmaartencarnival.com*.

dian house and features the history and culture of the island. Displays include artifacts from prehistoric to modern times.

Sint Maarten's proximity to other islands give vacationers the opportunity to visit **Anguilla** by ferry or take a hopper flight to **Saba** or **St. Eustatius**. Explore neighboring **St. Barts** with a quick trip aboard the Voyager 2, *Tel.*

011/590-87-10-68,
www.voyager-st-barths.com,
which departs from Marigot
to Gustavia, St. Barts at 9am
and 6:15pm daily (reservations required for Sunday departure). The 90-minute trip
aboard the high-speed boat is

comfortable, air conditioned,
and includes a stocked bar.

Casino gambling is a top activity on the Dutch side of the
island. Here's your chance to
enjoy slots and table games;
the atmosphere is fun and relaxed at all the casinos.

BEST SHOPPING

On the French side, the best
shopping is in the capital city
of **Marigot**. The **Marigot Market**, located on the docks, is
an open-air market scheduled
for every Wednesday and Saturday. It's a good chance to
experience a slice of local life
as residents shop for fresh fish
and fruit as well as spices.
The market continues up to
the ferry area, where vendors
sell items daily from kiosks
aimed at the tourist market:
woodcarvings, Haitian paintings, batik pareos, jewelry,
and more. Marigot is also
home to the West Indies Mall,
featuring fashion and jewelry
shops.

On the Dutch side,
Philipsburg is the best shop-
ping stop. Here shops line
Front Street, the narrow bou-

levard nearest the waterfront.
In these duty-free stores, electronic goods, leather, jewelry,
and liquor (especially
guavaberry liqueur) are especially good buys. (For the best
prices, shop on days when
the cruise ships are not in
port.) **No duties are charged
in or out of port** (one of the
few such ports in the world),
so savings run about 25-50%
on consumer goods at this
popular duty-free stop. Shop
carefully, though, and know
prices on specific goods before you leave home. Some
items are not such bargains.

Typically, shops open at 8 or
9am and remain open until
noon, then reopen from 2 to 6
daily. When cruises ships are
in port, most shops remain
open through the lunch hours.

BEST SPORTS & RECREATION

There's plenty of action on St. Maarten's shores; the brochures like to say 37 beaches, one for each of the island's 37 square miles. There's no denying that St. Martin's beautiful beaches are among this island's top assets. Whether you're looking for pulsating action or blissful privacy, you'll find it somewhere on the island.

On the French side, topless sunbathing is standard and nudity is permitted on the nude beach at Orient Bay. Best beaches include:

• **Long Bay** (Baie Longue). As its name suggests, this is the largest beach in St. Martin. From here you can walk west to Plum Bay, a shadier stretch of sand.

• **Grand Case Bay**. Located right in downtown Grand Case, this beach is relaxed and a good place to cool off after a midday meal.

• **Little Cayes**. One of the most isolated, this beach can only be reached by boat or by a 30-minute walk from Cul de Sac along a coastal trail.

• **Galion Beach**. These protected waters make them a favorite with beginning windsurfers and snorkelers.

• **Orient Bay** (*photo below*). The liveliest place on the entire island, the spot to see and be seen. This long stretch of powdery sand is lined with beach bars, restaurants, and watersports operators. Chaise loungers and umbrellas are available for rent all along the beach. The nudist area is located on the east side in front of Club Orient; photography is prohibited there.

• **Baie Rouge**. Swimmers find good conditions at this quiet hideaway.

SPORTS & RECREATION

SPORTS & RECREATION

• **Coconut Grove.** Families and snorkelers enjoy placid waters at this shady beach.
• **Baie de l'Embouchure.** Protected by a coral reef, these waters are good for sailing and windsurfing.
• **Baie Lucas.** Good diving from a shady beach here.

On the Dutch side, you'll find excellent beaches as well. Some of the best are:

• **Mullet Bay Beach** is perfect for swimming and snorkeling in gentle, protected waters although it is located adjacent to a presently deserted property.
• **Maho Beach** offers a totally different type of experience, with sometimes rough waters and the dubious thrill of watching planes coming in for a landing at Princess Juliana International Airport just over your head.
• **Cupecoy Beach**, located near the border with the French side. This is the beach you'll often see in Sint Maarten brochures, featuring beautiful sea caves carved in the cliffs and offering silhouetted views of aquamarine waters against sunflower toned sand. Many visitors come here to enjoy privacy and topless bathing. To reach the beach, go down the concrete stairs (uneven so watch out) located near the parking area at Sapphire Beach Club or continue down the dirt road past Sapphire, park at the end of the road, and walk down. This route takes you closest to the sea caves for which Cupecoy is noted.
• **Little Bay Beach** is a favorite with snorkelers. Calm waters mean good visibility except during a southeasterly wind.
• **Dawn Beach**, on the island's east side, is a favorite with wavehoppers and surf lovers. These waters can occasionally be too choppy for swimming and too churned up for good snorkeling, but this beach has one of the island's best sunrise views.
• **Oyster Pond** is where the legendary Frenchman and Dutchman started their walk around the island to divide the acreage between the two nations. Today the boundary makes an added attraction for beachlovers: you can swim between the French and Dutch sides in just a few strokes.

With such an array of beaches, it's not surprising that you'll find just about every type of

activity as far as **watersports** goes. Waverunners, catamarans, jet skis, parasailing, waterskiing, windsurfing, banana rides, beach toys, whatever. Watersports action is found primarily at Cupecoy Beach and Simpson Bay, a calm body of water popular with water-skiers. Boogie boarders head to Guana Bay, where shallows often have an undertow.

St. Maarten offers **scuba diving** for first timers and advanced divers. Visibility ranges from 75 to 125 feet in these waters which are home to a wide array of marine life. Waters are warm year around, averaging 70 degrees. One popular site is the wreck of the British man-o-war *Proselyte*, located on a reef a mile offshore. The 1801 wreck is located off Great Bay and still reveals its anchors and cannons. Another popular wreck dive is the *Teigland*, a freighter deliberately sunk in 1993. Located on Cable Reef, the site is home to many marine animals.

On the French side, top dive sites include Ilet Pinel, a shallow dive on the island's northeast coast near Orient Bay, Green Key, a barrier reef also near Orient Bay, and Flat Island (or Ile Tintamarre), known for its quiet coves and sub-sea geological faults. Anse Marcel, on the north side of the island, is another popular choice.

Good visibility makes **snorkeling** popular. A top snorkel spot on the Dutch side is Little Bay Beach, with good reefs and calm waters except during a southeast wind. On the French side, Orient Bay, Green Key, Ilet Pinel and Flat Island (Tintamarre) are classified as regional underwater nature reserves or Réserve Sous-Marine Régionale and are thus protected.

SPORTS & RECREATION

Snapper, grouper, yellowtail, sailfish, kingfish, tuna, mahi mahi, wahoo, shark, barracuda and marlin are the goal of **deep-sea charters** available on a half or full day basis year around. Good fishing is found not far offshore so anglers don't need to spend a lot of time traveling.

BEST SLEEPS & EATS

FRENCH ST. MARTIN
Esmeralda Resort $$$

From the action packed waters off Orient Beach, the green roofs of Esmeralda Resort are easy to spot. Eighteen villas, accommodating 65 guest rooms, are sprinkled across the low rise hills that rise up from Baie Orientale. Each villa includes its own swimming pool; accommodations offer air-conditioning, satellite TV, telephones, fully equipped kitchenettes, and private terraces. A poolside restaurant, L'Astrolabe, offers continental cuisine. *Info: Tel. 011/590-590-8736-36, www.esmeralda-resort.com.*

La Samanna Resort & Spa $$$$

This 81-room resort (*photo below*) is often cited as one of the Caribbean's most luxurious. This resort features rooms with cool white interiors, bamboo and mahogany furniture, and a genteel atmosphere. Along with the resort's Elysees Spa, La Samanna is

SLEEPS & EATS

also noted for its fine dining. *Info: Tel. 800/854-2252 or 011/590-590-8764-00, www.lasamanna.com.*

Radisson St. Martin Resort, Marina & Spa $$$$
Formerly operated as L'Habitation de Lonvilliers, the resort underwent an $80 million renovation and now includes 63 suites and 189 guest rooms, a 150-slip marina, full service spa, and more. *Info: Tel. 800/395-7046 or 011/590-590-8767-00, www.radisson.com/stmartin.*

The Rainbow $$$
Located on the waterfront, this fine restaurant is one to save for your most special night out. With Continental and French dishes, this eatery is the kind of place you will talk about long after your vacation. *Info: Grand Case, Tel.011/ 590-87-55-80.*

Kontiki $$$
As its name suggests, this casual beach eatery takes a Polynesian approach, sort of a Gilligan's Island meets St. Tropez. You can't miss the big Easter Island-type statues at the beachside entrance. Inside, however, the menu is strictly French. *Info: Orient Beach, Tel. 011/590-874327.*

DINING ON THE FRENCH SIDE

French St. Martin offers all types of cuisine. French food reigns but you'll also find Italian, Swiss, and many other types. Reservations usually aren't necessary at lunch, but plan ahead for dinner, especially during busy winter months. Prices for a three-course meal without wine are pricey. A good guide to local restaurants is *Ti Gourmet*, a free publication in French and English available from area hotels and the Tourist Office.

La Vie En Rose $$$
Diners can enjoy an elegant meal in the upstairs restaurant of this French eatery or a traditional French experience at the sidewalk cafe. *Info: Marigot, Tel. 011/590-87-54-42.*

SLEEPS & EATS

DUTCH SINT MAARTEN
Holland House $$

This Philipsburg hotel is the ideal location for serious shoppers. Especially popular with Dutch travelers in town to do business in Philipsburg, this charming European-style, 54-room hotel is also perfect for those who are looking to do a little business of their own in the duty-free shops. The hotel has undergone an extensive renovation and sports a South Beach meets the Caribbean vibe with a great lounge that faces Great Bay and the Philipsburg boardwalk. *Info: Tel. 011/599-542-2572, www.hhbh.com.*

Sonesta Great Bay Beach Resort & Casino $$-$$$

Located 10 minutes from downtown Philipsburg, this 257-room hotel offers visitors plenty of beachside fun. Daytime activities

include watersports (wave runners, sailboats, windsurfing, snorkeling, paddleboats), tennis, beach, and two swimming pools. Most visitors opt for the all-inclusive plan (although if you choose the room-only plan, you'll will find numerous restaurants of Philipsburg just a short walk away down the beach.) We've stayed at this property several times and can highly recommend it for families as well as couples. Our last stay was in a newly-renovated, two-bedroom suite with a kitchen. *Info: Tel. 011/599-54-22446, 800/SONESTA, www.sonesta.com/GreatBay.*

Sonesta Maho Beach Resort & Casino $$-$$$

This 534-room hotel, part of the Sonesta chain, is a high-rise built around a sprawling freshwater pool. Rooms are divided among two towers and vacationers find plenty of dining option as well as four tennis courts, two pools, and beach fun. We recommend the all-inclusive plan; longer stays include not only the restaurants on site but also several nearby restaurants. The resort, which offers around the clock fun, is the most convenient in terms of airport accessibility. You'll just be minutes from the airport—perfect for making the most of your vacation time and minimizing time in Philipsburg's often snarled traffic. Excellent dining options, nightclubs, and a large casino make this Sint Maarten's hottest nightspot. *Info: Tel. 011/599-545-2115, 800/SONESTA; www.sonesta.com.*

The Westin St. Maarten, Dawn Beach Resort & Spa $$$$
The largest infinity edge pool in St. Maarten reflects the facade of this 314-guest room retreat located on beautiful Dawn Beach.

Vacationers can relax on Heavenly Beds before embarking on an island adventure. Soak up some rays on the beach, then sign up for aquatic activities offered by the resort's dive operator, try out the gaming tables at the casino or unwind at the spa. *Info: Tel. 800/937-8461, 011/599-543-6700, www.starwoodhotels.com/westin.*

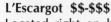

Le Bec Fin $$
This seaside restaurant has a casual downstairs eatery for breakfast and lunch and an upstairs section for an elegant dinner. Grilled lobster flambée, marinated duck breast, soufflés, and more tempt evening visitors. The lunch crowd enjoys quiche, burgers, fish sandwiches, and Neptune salads with sea scallops, smoked salmon, and marinated fish. *Info: Frontstreet, Philipsburg, Tel. 011/599-544-3930.*

L'Escargot $$-$$$
Located right on busy Front-

DINING ON THE DUTCH SIDE
Dutch Sint Maarten doesn't often receive the rave restaurant reviews awarded to French St. Martin, but that's a mistake. With culinary offerings that range from French to Indonesian to Italian, this part of the island offers excellent dining at prices that are often better than those found at restaurants in the French section. Restaurants throughout the island reflect the many cultures that live on this island and the many lands that the Netherlands once influenced.

street, this French eatery features, you guessed it, escargot. Try the snails in garlic butter, in cherry tomatoes, baked in mushroom caps, or cooked up in an omelet. Seafood includes yellowtail filet sautéed in lemon butter, snapper in red wine sauce and shallots, and lobster. The specialty dish is Le Canard de "L'Escargot", a crisp duck in pineapple and banana sauce and winner of an award from Gourmet magazine. *Info: 84 Frontstreet, Philipsburg. Tel. 011/599-542-2483, www.lescargotrestaurant.com.*

Rancho Argentinean Grill $$-$$$

Housed in a thatched roof building, this large restaurant serves up Argentinean delights. Start with sangria or wine and some *empanadas* or *chorizos criollos* (Argentinean grilled sausage) and continue with the house specialty: steak. Sirloin, tenderloin, rib eye and T-bone served with side orders such as *cebollas fritas* (fried onions), *maiz choclo* (grilled corn on the cob), *arroz criollo* (seasoned rice), or *plantos fritos* (fried plantains) make for a genuine Argentinean meal. *Info: Simpson Bay, Tel. 011/ 599-545-3098.*

Saratoga $$$

Located right at the yacht club, this elegant restaurant features an ever-changing menu that highlights local ingredients. Start with Wild Mushroom Bisque of Fish soup with Rouille and Gruyere Cheese and then select a main course: Grilled Mahi-Mahi with Whole Grain Mustard Sauce, Sautéed Red Snapper Fillet with Garlic-White Wine Butter Sauce, or Grilled Duck Breast with Duck Confit, Basmati Rice, and Yellow Roast Yellow Pepper Sauce. *Info: Simpson Bay Yacht Club, Tel. 011/ 599-544-2421.*

Wajang Doll $$

Rijstaffel is the order of the day at this delightful eatery that serves up delicious Indonesian dishes to satisfy even the pickiest of eaters. Choose from a 14- or 19-dish spread. Rijsttafel or "rice table", is an Indonesian feast that creates an evening of entertainment. Come with a big appetite to this spread. The meal begins with an appetizer of egg rolls followed by main courses such as *sateh ajam*, skewered chicken covered with a spicy peanut-flavored sauce, *kerrie djawa* (beef curry), *daging ketjap* (beef braised in soy and ginger sauce), and *telor* (egg in spiced coconut sauce.) Dinner only. *Info: Philipsburg, Tel. 011/ 599-544-2255.*

AMERICA'S CUP

Let's get this straight. We're not boaters. But we would name this boat race as one of our most exciting activities in the Caribbean. Our boat: the *Stars and Stripes* (yes, the same one that brought Dennis Conner to glory.) Our mission: to win the America's Cup.

Well, maybe not THE America's Cup. This is the **12-Metre Challenge**, *www.12metre.com,* a race for both first-time sailors and salty skippers alike, held three times daily, six days a week from the Philipsburg marina. We learned that this was no pleasure cruise — we were there to work. For the better part of an hour we practiced our jobs, tacking and jibing, kicking up a salty spray and often leaning so far into the wind that half the crew enjoyed a cool Caribbean bath.

The division of labor was spread among the crew. A navigator kept us on the course (which ranges from 8 to 12 miles, depending on wind conditions that day). A timekeeper ensured that we started the race without penalty. A hydraulics expert operated the hydraulic primer to control the boom and keep the sails tight. Backstay grinders and trimmers moved sails and ropes, as did mainsail grinders and trimmers.

With the wind whipping as hard as 20 knots and swells churning up at six feet, we were quickly dowsed as we turned into position. "Red flag up! Start!" The race was on. We were now on course, racing upwind and zigzagging through the eye of the wind by tacking as fast as the crew could shout orders.

Minutes later, we jibed around the windmark and began sailing downwind. *Canada II* had pulled into the lead, but we were just a boat length behind. From our position we could see the masts, the height of an eight story building, leaning into the wind.

For 45 minutes, we edged both Canadian vessels for the lead. Finally, on the last stretch, *Stars and Stripes* pulled ahead. With one last "Primary grinders, go!" instruction, we were leading.

And suddenly, there was one last shout. "Blue flag up!" Blue for *Stars and Stripes*. We had won.

Dennis would have been proud.

PRACTICAL MATTERS

Currency. The official currency for the French side is the Euro; the Dutch side uses the Netherlands Antilles guilder. However, US dollars are accepted on both sides of the island.

Getting There. Air service is available at two airports on the island: Princess Juliana International Airport on Dutch St. Maarten and L'Esperance Airport in Grand Case on the French side. The French airport is served only by a few commuter flights from St. Barts and Guadeloupe and private planes. Most travelers arrive in Dutch Sint Maarten at the newly expanded airport. Travel time to the island from is 2 1/2 hours from Miami, 3 1/2 from New York, 4 1/2 from Dallas, 5 from Montreal, and 8 hours from Paris.

Information. For information on Dutch Sint Maarten: *Tel. 800/ STMAARTEN*. For information on the French side: *Tel. 646/227- 9440 or 590/0-590-87-57-21*.

Websites. *www.vacationstmaarten.com* (Dutch side) and *www.st-martin.org* (French side).

15. TURKS & CAICOS

Ever wonder what it's like to discover a Caribbean hideaway? An island bathed in tropical pastels, where the sound of lapping surf fills the warm air with the promise of a walk on a chalk-white beach or a dive in turquoise waters filled with fish as colorful as a candy store window?

You'll feel like the two of you have made a lucky discovery in the **Turks and Caicos** (pronounced kay-cos), an archipelago of nearly 40 islands. Here you'll find over 200 miles of pristine beaches, a coral reef system spanning over 65 miles, and a group of islands that offers everything from late night roulette in an elegant casino to Robinson Crusoe-type solitude on uninhabited islands.

INTRO

The **Turks and Caicos** islands are located 1-1/2 hours from Miami, tucked halfway between the tip of Florida and Puerto Rico. This British crown colony, ruled by a governor appointed by the Queen, is better known in the world of banking than by travelers. With its tax-free status and with the stability of the British government backing the islands, the Turks and Caicos has offered off-shore banking for American corporations for many years.

The same attributes that make these islands so attractive to businesses also make them appealing to travelers. Daily jet service speeds travel. Once there, transport around the islands is easy, although conducted on the left side of the road.

You'll arrive in **Providenciales**, better known as simply Provo. This island is home to the largest portion of the Turks and Caicos population and to most hotel properties—none over three stories tall by law.

Some scholars of Christopher Columbus say that the Turks and Caicos island of Grand Turk may have been the island the explorer called "Guanahani," his first point of landfall in the New World. Although this early history remains unknown, historians are sure that these islands had a raucous and rollicking past as pirates' hideouts. Pirates from Bermuda settled **Grand Turk** and lured ships onto the coral reefs just offshore, plundering the ships even down to their wood timbers. Many historic buildings on Grand Turk were constructed from this pillaged lumber.

Although cotton was unsuccessful in these dry islands, the harvesting of sea salt remained a major industry until the middle of the 1900s. On the island of **Salt Cay**, you'll see the ruins of salt "pens" just as the workers left them decades ago with stockpiles of salt still heaped in decaying buildings.

Although the chain is composed of nearly 40 limestone islands, only eight are considered destinations. Providenciales is home to about 6000 residents and to most of the tourist industry. The capital of the Turks and Caicos is the island of Grand Turk, a short hop from Provo. This seven-mile square island has some historic buildings and the national museum, a must-see for history buffs.

Other inhabited islands include **North Caicos**, the most verdant island in the chain; **South Caicos**, a fishing center; **Middle Caicos**, home of several sea caves; and Salt Cay, a tiny island of only 300 residents that was once the world's largest producer of sea salt.

The ease of getting around the Turks and Caicos depends on the island you're visiting; Provo has the most travel options. Rental cars are available, but they can be expensive so some visitors opt for a car for just part of their stay. Taxi service is easier although, especially on smaller islands, you may have to call a taxi company and arrange for pickup.

BEST SIGHTS IN TURKS & CAICOS

With the number of tourists relatively low, you'll find that the number of attractions are equally sparse. Don't expect the shopping of St. Thomas or the reggae clubs of Jamaica or the submarine rides of Grand Cayman at this destination. For most travelers, the real attraction is being able to do nothing at all. Days are spent on the beach or in the water that's so clear it's often cited as the world's top scuba destination.

One unique attraction is the **Conch Farm**, Providenciales, Tel. 649/946-2160, the only farm in the world that raises Queen conch, the shellfish that's become a favorite meal throughout much of the Caribbean. On a guided tour, you'll see conch in various stages, from the larvae in the hatchery to juveniles about 4mm in length, to adulthood.

History buffs will find reason enough to take a day trip to Grand Turk to visit the **Turks and Caicos National Museum**, Grand Turk, www.tcmuseum.org; Tel. 649/946-2160. We think this is one of the most fascinating museums in the entire Carib-

SIGHTS

bean. The main exhibit features the **Molasses Reef shipwreck**, which occurred in the Turks and Caicos nearly 500 years ago. The Spanish caravel hit the reef and quickly sank in only 20 feet of water where it remained until the 1970s. Once excavated, it was recognized as the oldest European shipwreck in the New World.

The museum, located in a 150-year old house on the island's main street, features artifacts from the wreck with interactive displays, video presentations, and scientific exhibits. The name of this wrecked ship was never learned because, like drug-running planes of today, this was a ship with an illegal booty. Kept off the official records of Spain, the ship was

BEST FESTIVAL

The **Turks and Caicos Music and Cultural Festival** (TCMCF) has quickly developed into the nation's largest festival with live music and concerts, a boat regatta and cultural events. Spanning a week in late July/early August, the festival features internationally-known names from the music world; past performers have included Lionel Richie, LL Cool J, Alicia Keys, John Legend, Kenny Rogers, Michael Bolton, T.I., Shaggy, Ludacris, Anita Baker, and more. The event also features the Miss Turks and Caicos pageant. The festival is staged at the Turtle Cove Marina in Providenciales.

carrying slaves probably bound for the plantations of nearby Hispaniola.

BEST SHOPPING

Shopping in **Provo** has improved over the past few years but is still very limited. Don't expect to see duty free shops and boutiques on this island but you will find several small shopping areas that offer a selection of gift items, liquors, and travel necessities.

There is a shopping complex in Provo called **Ports of Call**, designed to resemble an old Caribbean seaside town. Look for restaurants, crafts and art in this development near Grace Bay. Several artists' galleries stand out for

SHOPPING

unique purchases. **Bamboo Gallery** at **Caicos Café Plaza**, *Tel. 649/946-4748*, features local and Haitian art.

Conch (pronounced Konk) shells make a wonderful souvenir from these islands. Stop by the **Conch Farm** to purchase a beautiful shell.

BEST SPORTS & RECREATION

Scuba diving and **snorkeling** are the top attractions of these islands. Visibility ranges from 80 to 100 feet or better and water temperatures hover at about 82 degrees in the summer and 75 or so in the winter months. Beneath the calm waves swim colorful marine animals as exotic as hawksbill turtles, nurse sharks, and octopus. With a one-mile vertical coral wall located offshore, Provo is a diver's paradise.

From December through April, ecotourists journey to Salt Cay for a chance to spot **humpback whales**, watching for the giant mammals from shore or in the water in scuba gear.

Visitors can enjoy bird watching on North Caicos or watching gentle rock iguanas on **Little Water Cay**, home of a new nature trail program, one of 33 nature reserves and refuges in the Turks and Caicos.

You'll enjoy watching the **iguanas** in their natural habitat from raised boardwalks and observation towers. Trips to Little Water Cay are offered by several operators who also schedule full-day excursions to the inhabited but sparsely developed islands of North and Middle Caicos for viewing a pink flamingo colony, talking with local residents,

and enjoying a beach barbecue.

Monthly **"glow worm"** cruises are another unique experience for travelers. Scheduled from three to six nights after a full moon, these cruises take visitors to the Caicos Bank for a look at phosphorescent marine worms that light the waters about an hour after sunset in a unusual mating ritual.

BEST SLEEPS & EATS

Amanyara $$$$
Wood and glass pavilions, each identical in layout, make up this stylish resort on Providenciales's Northwest Point. Each accom-

modation features sliding glass walls that open up to enjoy the sea breeze. The exclusive resort includes the Serenity Villa, a spa and wellness facility, plus tennis, a fitness center, beach club, library, pool, restaurant, and bar. *Info: Tel. 866/941-8133 or* 649/941-8133, www.amanyara.com.

Beaches Turks and Caicos Resort & Spa $$$-$$$$
Part of the Sandals family of resorts, this all-inclusive is a favorite with families. Located on the 12-mile beach at Grace Bay, the resort underwent a $125 million expansion to create the new Italian Village at Beaches Turks & Caicos. This section features 162 family suites with separate kids' rooms...and for the ultimate in luxury there are 18 Imperial Rooms with separate living room and dining room areas—not to mention butler service.

The expansion also features a private check-in area; five additional gourmet restaurants, bringing the resort's total to 16

SLEEPS & EATS

eateries; a sprawling retail mecca; and brand new amenities geared towards teens including teen-hang-out Trenchtown, complete with pool, air hockey and foosball tables, an aqua-themed night

club, *Liquid*, DJ-training sessions at Scratch DJ Academy and tailored spa treatments at the exclusive Red Lane® Spa. A newly renovated Pirate's Island Waterpark – ten times its original size – features a surf simulator, lazy river and seven new waterslides. *Info: Tel. 888/BEACHES or 649/946-8000, www.beaches.com.*

Grace Bay Club $$$$

Provo's first luxury resort, this all-suites hotel remains a tranquil oasis. The property is divided into the adults-only hotel area with

its own restaurant, pool, and bars and the family-friendly villa area with its own dedicated facilities. A unique feature is the Infiniti Bar, the longest bar in the Caribbean which

stretches for over 90 feet. *Info: Tel. 800/946-5757 or 649/946-5050, www.gracebayclub.com.*

Ocean Club Resorts $$-$$$$

This Provo resort grew from one to two excellent resort properties: Ocean Club and Ocean Club West. The two are less than a mile (or a 15-minute beach walk) apart and guests at one property enjoy the facilities of the other as well. Both of these all-suites properties are located on Grace Bay. *Info: Tel. 649/946-5880, 800/457-8787, www.oceanclubresorts.com.*

Parrot Cay $$$$

A favorite getaway for the rich and famous, Parrot Cay has also made headlines for several recent red carpet weddings including

the nuptials of Ben Affleck and Jennifer Garner. It's easy to see why Hollywood's elite opt for this getaway as a wedding spot or the location for their own home (or, like Bruce Willis, choose to say "I do" *and* get a second house here). The resort is home to a one-mile-long powdery beach and a full list of accommodations options, from rooms and suites to villas and even those Hollywood homes, if they're in the rental pool. The resort can arrange any type of activity you choose before your visit but for many, peace and privacy are the choice attractions. *Info: Tel. 877/754-0726 or 649/946-7788, www.parrotcay.como.bz.*

Anacaona $$$

Save one night for a special dinner at Anacaona, an Indian word that translates into "feather of gold." This open-air restaurant is true gold, a gem of a property that combines European elegance with Caribbean tranquility. The two of you can enjoy an elegant meal beneath a thatched palapa which rests on Roman columns. The menu is complemented with an extensive wine list and Cuban cigars. Reservations recommended. *Info: Grace*

T&C CUISINE

With the high number of both American visitors and expatriates, you'll find many cuisines represented on the islands. For a real taste of island food, sample the conch, served as fritters, salad, and sandwiches, as well as grouper, hogfish, soft-shell crab, and spiny lobster.

Bay Club, Providenciales, Tel. 800/946-5757 or 649/946-5050, www.gracebayclub.com.

Smokey's on the Bay $$
Popular with locals for seafood platters, this casual restaurant offers some good prime rib, cracked conch, pan fried or broiled grouper. Open for lunch and dinner daily except Sunday. *Info: Blue Hills, Providenciales, Tel. 649/241-4343.*

Tiki Hut $$
This casual restaurant starts the day with Gran Marnier croissant French toast, Belgian waffles, tropical pancakes, and it gets better from there. Look for favorites including conch fritters, conch chowder, West Indian chicken, Caribbean jerk pork chops, and more. *Info: Turtle Cove Marina, Providenciales, Tel. 649/941-5351, www.tikihuttci.com.*

PRACTICAL MATTERS

Currency. The US dollar is the official currency.

Driving. Driving is on the LEFT.

Getting There. Most visitors to the Turks and Caicos arrive on Providenciales (there is a smaller airport on Grand Turk). Service from Miami is available from major US airlines. Flying time to Providenciales is about 80 minutes from Miami or two and a half hours from Atlanta. To island hop, book a seat aboard an inter-island charter flights with Air Turks and Caicos, *Tel. 649/946-4181, www.airturksandcaicos.com*, or Global Airways, *Tel. 649/941-3232, www.globalairways.tc.* Charter boat transfers are another option.

Information. Turks and Caicos Tourist Board, *Tel. 866/413-8875, 646/375-8830; www.turksandcaicostourism.com.*

16. U.S. VIRGIN ISLANDS

A trip to the **U.S. Virgin Islands** is truly "no problem" because you never leave American soil. No passport needed for US citizens. No need to change money. No need to buy foreign postage stamps. You're still at home, but, oh, what a beautiful home it is.

And also a uniquely different home. While still a part of the US, the US Virgin Islands are a special mix of American and Caribbean. English is spoken but with a distinct Caribbean lilt called calypso. Driving is on the left side of the road. And restaurant menus feature a few items that you may not recognize (but you must try.)

License plates proudly proclaim that this is "America's Paradise." It's America's own vacationland, a place for lovers to enjoy some of the greatest duty-free shopping, dance to a Caribbean beat, swim in some of the region's clearest waters, or do some "limin'," the Virgin Islanders' word for just kicking back and enjoying a taste of paradise.

INTRO

The US Virgin Islands offer three distinct vacations. Shoppers and high-energy types will love **St. Thomas**, where poinciana-covered hills overlook streets filled with some of the Caribbean's finest duty-free shopping, one of the region's busiest cruise ship ports, and some of the most luxurious resorts in the isles.

Next door, tiny **St. John** is custom-made for nature lovers, who can camp and hike in the national park which covers two-thirds of this unspoiled island, and villa fans who can enjoy a home away from home experience in one of the island's multi-million dollar villas.

And, last but largest, **St. Croix** enchants travelers with its small town charm, picturesque Danish architecture, and one of the Caribbean's finest snorkeling trails.

Island hopping is part of life here. St. Thomas and St. John are just a 20-minute ferry ride apart, and it's just another short hop over to the British Virgin Islands, a very popular day trip. (You will need a passport to go to and return from the BVI.) Forty miles to the south, St. Croix is connected to its sister islands by 25-minute flights or by high-speed catamaran.

Taxis are easy to obtain. In Christiansted on St. Croix, stop by the taxi stand on King Street, in Frederiksted the taxi stand is at Fort Frederik. Licensed taxi services bear a license plate that begins with "TP." In St. Thomas, taxis are parked at the Vendors' Market. All taxi fares are fixed and, by law, taxis must carry a list of the fixed fares.

Rental cars are readily available; all you'll need is a valid U.S. driver's license. Driving, however, is on the left side of the road.

 ## BEST SIGHTS IN THE U.S.V.I.

St. Croix

The center of activity on St. Croix is the town of **Christiansted**, just minutes from where Columbus originally landed and named this island Santa Cruz. (Today residents born on St. Croix are known as Crucians.) Looking like a building carved from lemon sherbet, the **Old Scalehouse** once weighed sugar, the product of over 100 stone mills scattered across the island in the late 19th century. The sugar was loaded

SIGHTS

SIGHTS

on ships that later returned to St. Croix with a ballast of brick, used to construct many of the homes and businesses. Near the Old Scalehouse, **Fort Christianvaern** is now operated by the U.S. Park Department. The yellow fortress, with its dungeons and old cannons, is now open for self-guided tours.

As appealing as Christiansted's charms are, the real beauty of the island lies beyond the city limits. Here, on rolling hills littered with historic sugar mills, the island takes on a country charm. Bucolic cattle dot open fields, small homes cling to the hillsides along winding roads, and the occasional shy mongoose, imported to kill snakes, scampers like a large squirrel across the road and under cover.

Traveling west from Christiansted, the island becomes progressively more lush. This natural abundance is best seen at the **St. George Botanical Gardens**, a 16-acre park (*photo above*) where 800 species of Caribbean plants thrive among the ruins of a sugar cane plantation. Bougainvillea as colorful as crepe

paper lines the walkways that lead visitors on a self-guided tour of an orchid house, a rain forest, and even a cactus garden.

The lavish lifestyle enjoyed by plantation owners during the 19th century is preserved at the **Whim Greathouse**. Here we toured an elegant home that combined English gentility with Caribbean practicality, filled with fine imported furniture as well as floor-to-ceiling shuttered windows and cool plank floors. If you're lucky, you'll be able to sample some freshly-made johnny cakes, baked in the plantation's detached cookhouse. (And don't miss the gift shop filled with Caribbean cookbooks, perfumes, and crafts.)

St. Croix's southern city, **Frederiksted**, lies just a few miles from the former plantation house. A stop for many cruise ships, the town is a smaller version of Christiansted with a red, rather than yellow, fortress guarding the waterfront.

St. Croix's best treasures, however, are not the man-made ones but the natural areas found at opposite ends of the island. From Frederiksted, take Rt. 76 or the Mahogany Road north for a trip to the **rainforest**. The small rainforest has thick vegetation where the sunlight is filtered through mahogany, yellow cedar, and Tibet trees. This forest is also home of **LEAP**, the Life and Environmental Arts Project, where skilled artisans craft everything from sculptures to spoons from the hardwoods found in the rain forest.

Just off the coast of the far northeast side of the island lies St. Croix's other natural treasure: **Buck Island**. Several outfitters take snorkelers on half- and full-day trips to this island to swim along the **Buck Island Reef National Monument**. Here, in about 12 feet of water, snorkelers follow a marked trail for a self-guided tour of this undersea world. Or would you like to be the first Americans to see the day's sunrise? On **Point Udall**, the easternmost spot in the territorial United States, the US first greets the sunrise. As dawn's rays bathe the Point in light, red Senapol cattle begin another day of grazing on nearby scrub-covered hills. Along a rocky shoreline, where even on the busiest days the sea-grape trees far outnumber the sunbathers, visitors find themselves virtually alone to enjoy daybreak an hour before it reaches the mainland. Point Udall is home to Point Udall Millennium Monument, built in 2000 to mark the spot where the first sunrise over the US of the millennium took place.

St. John

The biggest attraction of St. John is the national park. Start with a visit to the **Virgin Islands National Park Visitors Center**, located on the waterfront in Cruz Bay. Here you'll find information on hiking,

SIGHTS

camping, snorkeling, and guided programs.

After you have your bearings, head out to the park by taxi or rental jeep. Hike on one of the many marked trails, snorkel the **guided underwater trail** at Trunk Bay, stroll along the self-guided Cinnamon Bay Nature Trail, or visit ruins of Annaberg Sugar Plantation.

St. Thomas

Island tours are an excellent way to get an overview of St. Thomas. Most are conducted in open-air, safari-type buses and include pickup from your hotel and make scenic stops at Drake's Seat and Mountain Top. Check with your hotel for pick-up times. Another excellent view of **Charlotte Amalie** is from **the lookout on Skyline Drive**. Here all the guided tours stop for a quick photo. Your jitney tour will undoubtedly stop at Mountain Top, the peak of St. Peter Mountain. This lookout is home to a mega-gift shopping complex, mucho tourists, banana daiquiris (they claim to be the home of the original banana daiquiri), and, we must admit, a beautiful view. From the lookout, you'll have a great view of Tortola, Jost Van Dyke, and Magens Bay. Another way to enjoy a panoramic view is with a ride up the **Paradise Point Tramway** (*Tel. 340/774-9809*), just across the street from Havensight Mall and the cruise dock. At the top, you'll find a great view and a small cafe.

One of the most popular attractions on St. Thomas is **Coral World** (*Tel. 888/695-2073, www.coralworldvi.com*). The park is well worth several hours thanks to its numerous exhibits. The most noticeable feature is its Undersea Observatory, located 100 feet offshore and accessible by walkway. You'll descend stairs and have the chance to peek at life 15 feet beneath the surface (including a look at SeaTrek participants wearing helmets and walking on the sea floor.) Fish feeding is a draw at the Caribbean Reef Encounter exhibit, an 80,000-gallon tank filled with tropical fish and corals.

This exhibit is wheelchair accessible. There's also a Deep Reef tank, filled with the predators of the deep including shark and barracuda.

But only a portion of Coral World is behind glass; many of the exhibits are outdoors in the open air (so don't save this for a rainy day option; the outdoor activities are equally as fun as the indoor ones here.) Coral World is located on **Coki Beach**; your admission ticket means you can visit a while, hit the beach, then return to check out more exhibits or to catch a feeding time. Coki Beach is shallow and calm and good for young children.

St. Thomas's most famous beach is beautiful **Magens Bay**, a picture postcard-perfect beach where you'll find everything you need, from beach chairs to a beach bar, to allow you to luxuriate all day here.

BEST FESTIVALS

The biggest party of the year in **St. Thomas** is **Carnival**, the April celebration that brings the island alive with colorful parades, calypso, Mocko Jumbies, and dancing in the streets. It's a time when vacationers can party with islanders and celebrate during a whole month of activity.

Any visit to St. John is celebration enough, but during the summer the island parties with a purpose. In June, the **St. John Festival** celebrates the heritage of the island with pulsating parades, and live music.

St. Croix celebrates year around, reaching a crescendo with the **Crucian Christmas Festival**. This carnival festival begins the first Thursday in December and ends the first Saturday of the New Year. You'll find an adults' parade, children's parade, Jouvert, a festival village and more at this extensive event.

SIGHTS

BEST SHOPPING

Although it pales in comparison to its more cosmopolitan cousin, Charlotte Amalie on St. Thomas, **St. Croix's Christiansted** still boasts enough shops to keep even the most dutiful consumer happy. You'll find high dollar goods at duty-free shops known for Rolexes, crystal, and jewelry, as well as boutiques offering the finest of the world's perfume, china, and gold. However, some of the best buys are items that bring home the spirit of the Caribbean: the "St. Croix hook," a bracelet in gold or silver designed by **Sonya Lts.** (*No. 1 Company Street, Christiansted*), featuring a simple hook clasp that gives a clue to the wearer's romantic status: pointed down it signifies the wearer is single, pointed up and turned toward the heart it symbolizes attachment.

St. John offers a very different shopping experience than nearby St. Thomas. Duty-free shopping is available, but by far the emphasis here is on hand-made items: clothing, pottery, jewelry, and artwork.

The most concentrated shopping on St. John is found at **Mongoose Junction** in **Cruz Bay** across from the National Park dock. Here, look for batik fabrics, artists' galleries, home furnishings and other handicrafts.

Also in Cruz Bay, you'll find the **Donald Schnell Studio** offering fine ceramics with an island flair. The studio is located at **The Amoré Center**, *Tel. 800/253-7107 or 340/776-6420.* Schnell's signs, with their distinctive sea green glass numbers and letters, adorn many St. John villas.

St. Thomas is where serious duty-free shoppers come to seek out bargains from around the globe on jewelry, perfumes, leather goods, and gemstones.

The Waterfront Highway (Kyst Vejen), Main Street (Dronningens Gade) and Back Street (Vimmelskaft Gade) run parallel to the waterfront of **Charlotte Amalie**. These streets, and the alleys that connect Waterfront Highway and Main Street, are filled with non-stop shops. Start near the

SHOPPING

Vendor's Plaza (crafts purchases, inexpensive T-shirts), then begin your walk down crowded **Main Street**, where the sidewalks are always packed with shoppers and the street is continually lined with taxis and jitneys.

Our favorite shops are tucked in the alleys, refuges from the crowds where you can shop, dine or drink in a little peace. Here the walls are brick, recalling the area's history. In the 19th century, this was the Danish warehouse district.

BEST SLEEPS & EATS

ST. CROIX

The Buccaneer $$$

No other hotel in St. Croix , and few in the Caribbean, boasts the impressive history of The Buccaneer, located east of Christiansted. Once owned by Charles Martel, one of the Knights of Malta, the estate had walls three feet thick and was tucked just behind a hill to hide it from view of pirates. Later, the stately manor was the residence of the young Alexander Hamilton.

Today, the original estate is supplemented with modern rooms to complete the 138-room resort but the rich historic atmosphere remains. Every week, guests and staff come together at the manager's cocktail party, hosted in a stone sugar mill that stands as a reminder of the island's early plantation past.

History at the Buccaneer doesn't just end with the facilities — it extends to the resort owners as well. Today the ninth generation of the Armstrong family to reside on St. Croix operates the expansive resort.

The Buccaneer is also well-known for its sports facilities, especially tennis and golf. Eight tennis courts are located halfway down the hill from the main house. Golfers can take their best swing at an 18-hole course with views of the sea. Packages with unlimited golf are available. *Info: Tel. 800/255-3881 or 340/712-2100, www.thebuccaneer.com.*

Divi Carina Bay Beach Resort & Casino $$

Located on a quiet stretch on the south side of the island (you'll probably want to rent a car if you stay here), this resort boasts a

1,000-foot white sand beach that's one of its strongest points or you can also opt for a dip in one of the two pools. Beachside rooms are our favorite (larger villas are located across the road up on the hillside). Rooms are decorated in island style and all include coffee maker, refrigerator and microwave. The resort has a casino but it is set across the road from the main portion of the resort and doesn't intrude into the relaxed atmosphere of the property. *Info: Tel. 340/773-9700 or 877/773-9700, www.divicarina.com.*

DINING ON ST. CROIX

St. Croix has a wide variety of dining options, from gourmet restaurants to fast food chains. You'll find many cuisines represented here as well, including Caribbean, Italian, French, and, yes, Danish. Don't miss the **conch** here, it's an island specialty. The shellfish is often served with a side dish called **fungi** (pronounced foon-gee), a tasty accompaniment that's somewhat like cornbread dressing. The most popular beer here is Heineken.

Brass Parrot $$$

This is one of our favorite restaurants, both for its unsurpassed cuisine and for its unbeatable nighttime view of the lights of Christiansted twinkling in the distance. The glass-walled restaurant features a Northern Italian menu. *Info: The Buccaneer, Tel. 340/712-2100.*

Tutto Bene $$$

This Italian restaurant that's been praised by both *Gourmet* and *Bon Appetit* magazines is popular with locals and visitors alike. Favorites include beef or cheese ravioli, spinach lasagna, spaghetti carbonara, and veal marsala. Open for dinner daily; reservations suggested. *Info: Boardwalk Building Hospital Street, Gallows Bay, Tel. 340/773-5229.*

ST. JOHN
Caneel Bay $$$$
Caneel has the air of old-world Caribbean elegance that tells you, without a word, that this resort was a Laurance Rockefeller development. Tucked within the Virgin Islands National Park, Caneel boasts seven beaches and a natural beauty that is sur- passed only by the resort's high quality service. Spread out across the lush property, 166 cottages combine "casual elegance" with "St. John camping" to come up with a property where you can feel like you are camping while enjoying plenty of pampering. Cooled by trade winds and a ceiling fan, each cottage has furnishings from the Philippines, screened walls that are open to a pristine view, and cool terrazzo floors as well as an ice chest for daily ice delivery.

Guests check in when they arrive at the airport in St. Thomas and board private ferry service to the resort. (The ferry service is available several times daily so guests can hop to St. Thomas for a little shopping.) Private ferry service is also available three times a week to the resort's sister property, Little Dix Bay, on Virgin Gorda. Bring along your passport to take this jaunt to the British Virgin Islands.

Along with plenty of complimentary diversions (including the Peter Burwash International tennis program), introductory scuba diving clinic, windsurfing, Sunfish and kayaks, and movie presentations, other activities are avail- able at additional charge: half- and full-day sails, beach barbecue, sunset cocktail cruise, guided snorkel trips, fishing char

SLEEPS & EATS

ters, massages, and boat charters. However you choose to enjoy Caneel, there's one thing sure to please everyone: the resort's beaches. Here seven pristine stretches of sand are available, so guests can visit a different beach every day. Guests can hop aboard the resort shuttle for quick drop off at any of these beaches; don't forget to request a picnic lunch to take along! *Info: Tel. 888/ROSEWOOD or 340/776-6111, www.caneelbay.com.*

Harmony Studios $$

Don't let the fact that Harmony Studios is located at an "eco-resort" fool you: these accommodations are not camping. These apartments, located at Maho Bay Camps, were designed to be a resort in tune with nature. Solar power, recycled materials, low flush toilets, and a complete awareness of the environment makes this an eco-sensitive resort, but with a higher number of creature comforts than are found at its sister property, Maho. These units include energy-efficient refrigerators, a computer to track energy use, comfortable furnishings (a king-sized bed—roll-aways available—in the bedroom studio units or a king-sized bed and a queen-sized sofa bed in the living room studios), private baths, a deck with furniture, and kitchen. *Info: Tel. 340/715-0501 or 800/392-9004, www.maho.org.*

Westin St. John Resort & Spa $$$$

Like the turquoise waters of Great Cruz Bay, a stay at this 175-guest room, 146 villa resort can be a sea of tranquility or an ever-

moving adventure. Vacationers can enjoy a little pampering with a spa treatment, lounge on a white sand beach, perfect their putts at the nearby Mahogany Run 18-hole golf course, or dive into the deep with scuba instructors, embark on an Adventure Tour snorkeling excursion or try and try to reel in a whopper on a sport fishing trip. *Info: Tel. 340/693-8000. 866/716-8108 or 800/WESTIN-1, www.westinresortstjohn.com or www.starwoodhotels.com/westin.*

SLEEPS & EATS

For the most part, **dining on St. John** is a semi-casual affair, with restaurants featuring a continental mix to satisfy mainlander appetites.

Asolaré $$$
One of the best views is from the deck of Asolaré, an open-air restaurant featuring Asian fusion dishes served in a relaxed and romantic setting. *Info: Estate Lindholm Hotel, Tel. 340/779-4747.*

RENT A VILLA
St. John boasts a number of **exquisite private villas** for the ultimate in privacy. For brochures of these homes, many with private pools, contact a villa broker such as **McLaughlin Anderson**, *Tel. 800/537-6246 (St. Thomas) or 800/666-6246 (West Coast), www.mclaughlinanderson.com,* which we've used several times and enjoyed staying in several beautiful villas they represent.

Equator Restaurant $$$
Featuring cuisine from countries around the equator, this popular restaurant sets a global tone and is far more interesting than traditional hotel eateries. Designed with large beams that radiate across the circular, open-air dining room like longitudinal lines, the restaurant offers a great sunset view across the sea to St. Thomas. Highlights of the menu include Pepper-Cured Tandoori Lamb on Egyptian Cous Cous with

Mango-Pickles, Wok-Fried Whole Catfish with Polynesian Ponzu and Fried Rice, and Brazilian T-Bone Steak with Churrasco Sauce. Reservations are recommended. *Info: Caneel Bay, Tel. 340/776-6111.*

The Fishtrap Restaurant $$
This casual, open-air restaurant specializes in, you guessed it, fish. Start with shrimp cocktail, conch fritters, or Fish Trap chowder, then get serious with rock lobster tail, sea scallops,

shrimp scampi, or surf and turf. Burgers and pasta dishes including fettuccine alfredo with shrimp or scallops round out the menu. *Info: Cruz Bay, Tel. 340/693-9994, www.thefishtrap.com.*

Ocean Grill $$-$$$

Open for lunch and dinner daily except Sunday, this restaurant features favorites such as tempura scallops, grilled miso glazed ahi tuna, pan roasted Atlantic salmon, and more. *Info: Mongoose Junction, Cruz Bay, Tel. 340/693-3304, www.oceangrillstjohn.net.*

Sun Dog Cafe and Gecko Gazebo Bar $$

Take a break from your shopping at this casual eatery that features Tex-Mex, pizza, Mahi-Mahi sandwiches and more in what's been voted the best lunch spot on the island. *Info: Mongoose Junction, Cruz Bay, Tel. 340/693-8340, www.sundogcafe.com.*

ST. THOMAS
Marriott Frenchman's Reef & Morning Star Beach Resort $$$
The hotel-style Frenchman's Reef is popular with conventions and meetings but it also makes a fine place to vacation. We've stayed here several times and greatly enjoyed this property. Along with a good pool complex and beach, we enjoyed the water taxi service into Charlotte Amalie as well as the beautiful night views of the city from the resort.

Morning Star lies just down the hill from Frenchman's Reef and is ideal for vacationers who want to spend much of their time on the beach. Like Frenchman's Reef, the resort offers just about any activity you could select: sports, watersports (enjoyed right off the beach at this property), water taxi service into town, and more. However, here travelers can stroll right from their rooms to the beach. *Info: Tel. 340/776-8500 or 800/228-9290, www.marriott.com.*

The Ritz-Carlton, St. Thomas $$$$

Just as you would expect from a member of the Ritz-Carlton family, this resort is really grand. This is one of the most elegant hotels in the Caribbean, an ultra-luxurious resort designed to make its visitors feel like royalty. From the moment you enter the marble entry of this resort styled to replicate a Venetian palace, you'll know that this is a step above even the luxurious resorts for which the island is known. Maintaining a one-to-one guest to staff ratio, the resort is for those vacationers who are ready for privacy and pampering.

The hotel's hibiscus-colored roofs dot the shoreline of Great Bay. Here, amid stark white buildings punctuated with bougainvillea and other tropical splendors, await some of the island's most luxurious guest rooms. Marble baths, seersucker robes, and French doors leading out to private balconies greet guests. Away from their rooms, visitors continue to enjoy the finest in amenities, including sailing, snorkeling, and a private yacht. A private catamaran is used as a private guest shuttle to St. John. Fresh from a $47 million renovation, the resort recently added the Caribbean's first Prada Spa. *Info: Tel. 340/775-3333 or 800/241-3333, www.ritzcarlton.com.*

Wyndham Sugar Bay Resort & Spa $$$

This 294-room resort offers a real rarity in the US Virgin Islands: an all-inclusive option. With the all-inclusive plan, travelers can stay, play, and eat for one easy price. The all-inclusive package includes all meals and drinks, an ice cream bar, day and night tennis, all non-motorized watersports, use of snorkel equipment, use of fitness center and Jacuzzi, daily activity programs, nightly entertainment, and beach volleyball.

Much of the activity centers around the spectacular pool area. Here three interconnecting pools echo with the roar of a man-made waterfall. Visitors reach the pool area across a suspended bridge (look in the hibiscus for a resident iguana on the way down!) and a casual dining area lies just steps away. Beyond the pool area, the beach offers plenty of watersports and has some good snorkeling just yards from the shore, a site where we spotted about 40 small squid one afternoon. *Info: Tel. 340/777-7100 or 800/WYNDHAM, www.wyndham.com.*

DINING ON ST. THOMAS

Dining on St. Thomas can be elegant or casual. Just as its shops offer merchandise from around the globe, look for cuisine from many cultures represented here as well. Don't miss the local offerings, though: **fungi** (foon-gee), a side dish much like a cornbread stuffing, and **conch** (konk), the shellfish that's prepared as an entree or appetizer.

A Room with a View Wine Bar & Bistro $$$
Located at Bluebeard's Castle, this fine dining, dinner-only restaurant overlooks Charlotte Amalie and the harbor, making it one of the most romantic evening spots on the island. You'll typically find a catch of the day option here; a house specialty is Lobster Thermador. Chicken marsala and Duck L'Orange are also popular choices. *Info: Bluebeard's Castle, Tel. 340/774-2377, roomwithaviewvi.com.*

Gladys' Cafe $-$$
Popular with locals and visitors, this breakfast and lunch restaurant specializes in local fare. If you like conch, here's the place. Conch fritters, conch chowder, conch salad platter, conch in lemon butter sauce, you name it. Also look for sauté shrimp in lemon and garlic sauce. Don't miss the fungi. *Info: Royal Dane Mall West, Charlotte Amalie, Tel. 340/774-6604.*

PRACTICAL MATTERS

Currency. The US dollar is the official currency.

Driving. Driving is on the LEFT side of the road.

Getting to St. Thomas and St. Croix. Both St. Thomas and St. Croix are home to airports with extensive service at St. Croix's Henry E. Rohlsen International Airport and St. Thomas's Cyril E. King International Airport. From either airport, you'll need to take a taxi to your hotel. Hotels and resorts are not allowed to send a hotel van to pick up guests.

Take a day trip between St. Thomas and St. Croix with a quick hop between islands on the **seaplane**, which departs from downtown Christiansted and arrives in downtown Charlotte Amalie. Seaborne Seaplane, *Tel. 888/359-8687 or 340/773-6442, www.seaborneonline.com*, provides shuttle service between the two islands.

Getting To St. John. St. John does not have an airport, so you'll arrive by boat. Most visitors arrive via ferry service from either Red Hook or Charlotte Amalie, St. Thomas, *Tel. 340/776-6282*. From Red Hook, it's a 20-minute, one-way cruise. A private water taxi from Red Hook is a wonderful luxury; call Dohm's Water Taxi, *Tel. 340/775-6501, virginislandswatertaxi.com*.

Information. US Virgin Islands Division of Tourism, *Tel. 800/372-USVI or 340/774-8784*.

Website. *VisitUSVI.com*.

INDEX